# Wick's Punctuation Rules for Court Reporters

Kenneth A. Wick

Wick's Punctuation Rules
for Court Reporters
(August 2023)

# Table of Contents

## Numbers

# Introduction

The grading guidelines for the National Court Reporters Association state:

> The RSR, RPR and RMR skills tests are developed based on the rules of punctuation set forth in *The Gregg Reference Manual* and *Merriam Webster's Dictionary*.[1]

A Facebook poll showed 86 percent of court reporters use either *Morson's English Guide for Court Reporters* (Morson) or *Court Reporting: Bad Grammar / Good Punctuation* (Wells). Only 9 percent of court reporters use *The Gregg Reference Manual* (Gregg).[2] The low Gregg usage is probably the result of its focus: English composition. Morson and Wells focus on punctuating court reporting transcripts.

Unfortunately, Gregg, Morson, and Wells have not been updated in more than 10 years. Morson was last published in 1997, Gregg in 2011, and Wells in 2011. The punctuation and style rules in *Wick's Punctuation Rules for Court Reporters* are based on the most recent style guides:

- *The Gregg Reference Manual*[3]
- *The Chicago Manual of Style*[4]
- *The Redbook: A Manual on Legal Style*[5]
- *The Associated Press Stylebook*[6]
- *Merriam-Webster.com Dictionary* for spelling.

---

[1] "What is an Error? Grading Guidelines for the RSR, RPR and RMR Skills Tests", National Court Reporters Association, ncra.org, November 2019, accessed 31 May 2023, https://www.ncra.org/docs/default-source/uploadedfiles/certification/rsr-rpr-rmr-what-is-an-error.pdf.

[2] Poll results as of May 7, 2018. https://www.facebook.com/groups/ECRSgroup/permalink/10155054095880689/.

[3] *The Gregg Reference Manual*, 11th Edition, 2011.

[4] *The Chicago Manual of Style*, 17th Edition, 2017.

[5] *The Redbook: A Manual on Legal Style*, 4th Edition, 2018.

[6] *The Associated Press Stylebook, 56th Edition (2022-2024)*.

<u>Punctuation Mastery:</u>
The more grammar you know, the better your punctuation will be. You do not need to be a grammarian, but you cannot punctuate well without understanding **essential grammar** and **sentence structure**.

To punctuation well, you should be able to

- identify an **independent clause** (see G4).
- identify a **dependent clause** (see G5).
- identify a **subordinating conjunction** (see G6).
- identify a **coordinating conjunction** (see G7).
- identify a **conjunctive adverb** (see G8).
- identify a **transitional expression** (see G8).
- identify a **parenthetical expression** (see G9).
- identify a **prepositional phrase** (see G10).
- identify a **verbal phrase** (see G11)
- determine if a sentence element is **essential** or **nonessential** (see G12 and G13).
- identify and use the patterns of the four sentence types: **simple, compound, complex,** and **compound-complex** (see G26 to G32).

Therefore, before you rush straight to the punctuation and style rules, please thoroughly review the following:

1. **Essential Grammar.** Mastering grammar topics will greatly improve your punctuation. Read and then carefully study all essential grammar sections.

2. **Punctuation Overview.** Many punctuation rules are just the application of the punctuation mark's purpose. Knowing the basic purpose of each punctuation mark will help you remember and apply the rules.

3. **Sentence Types.** Knowing the four sentence types and any associated punctuation patterns will improve your punctuation because you will organize the transcript words into the sentence types and apply the punctuation patterns.

# Essential Grammar

## G1. English Parts of Speech
English has eight parts of speech.

| | |
|---|---|
| 1. Noun | A person (Jim), place (ocean), or thing (table) |
| 2. Pronoun | Substitute for a noun (he, she, it) |
| 3. Verb | Expresses action (to run) or state of being (is) |
| 4. Adjective | Describes a noun (big, red) |
| 5. Adverb | Describes a verb, adjective, or another adverb (slowly, not) |
| 6. Conjunction | Joins words, phrases, or clauses (and, but) |
| 7. Preposition | Connects a noun or pronoun to another word or sentence element (on, above, over) |
| 8. Interjection | Expresses feeling (wow, damn) |

## G2. English Word Order
The expected word order in an English sentence is subject, then verb, and then object.

| | |
|---|---|
| Verb: | What is the action? |
| Subject: | Who or what is doing the action? |
| Direct Object: | The who or what about the verb. |
| Indirect Object: | The to whom or for whom about the verb. |

- She kicked the ball.

| | |
|---|---|
| Verb (action): | kicked |
| Subject (who kicked?): | she |
| Direct Object (kicked what?): | the ball |
| Indirect Object (kicked to whom?): | (None) |

- I gave him money.

| | |
|---|---|
| Verb (action): | gave |
| Subject (who gave?): | I |
| Direct Object (gave what?): | money |
| Indirect Object (gave to whom?): | him |

## G3. Clauses and Phrases

A **clause** is a group of related words containing a subject and a predicate (verb plus any modifiers and complements). Clauses are classified as either a dependent clause or an independent clause (see G4 and G5).

A **phrase** is a group of related words without a subject, a predicate, or both. Two common phrase types are verbal phrases and prepositional phrases (see G10 and G11).

An **elliptical clause** is a grammatically incomplete clause that represents a complete clause (see G27). It lacks a subject, a predicate, or both. Any missing element is understood from the context.

## G4. Independent Clause

An independent clause is a clause (subject and predicate) that does <u>not</u> begin with a subordinating conjunction. It could stand alone as a simple sentence (see G26).

- Edward tripped.
- I paid the rent.
- Tim spent $1,000.

## G5. Dependent Clause

A dependent clause is a clause (subject and predicate) that begins with a subordinating conjunction (see G6). A dependent clause often describes an independent clause, and it can function as a noun, adverb, or adjective. It <u>cannot</u> stand alone as a simple sentence (see G26).

- Edward tripped **because he did not tie his shoe**.
- **When I received my paycheck**, I paid the rent.

A **relative clause** is a dependent clause that begins with a relative pronoun (that, who, which, whom, whose). A relative clause functions as an adjective.

- I live with a nice guy **who is my football teammate**.
- Tim spent $1,000 **that was for the rent**.

## G6. Subordinating Conjunctions

A subordinating conjunction begins and joins a dependent clause to an independent clause. See G31 for the three ways to join the dependent clause.

Common Subordinating Conjunctions:

| | | |
|---|---|---|
| **after** | inasmuch | till |
| although | in case | **though** |
| **as** | in case that | unless |
| as far as | in order | **until** |
| as if | in order that | **when** |
| as long as | lest | whenever |
| as soon as | now that | **where** |
| as though | once | whereas |
| **because** | only if | wherever |
| **before** | provided | **whether** |
| even if | provided that | **which** |
| even though | rather than | **while** |
| **how** | **since** | **who** |
| **if** | **so** | whoever |
| if only | so that | whom |
| if when | **than** | whomever |
| if then | **that** | whose |

- John made dinner **after** he went to the store.
  - Independent clause:  John made dinner
  - Dependent clause:    after he went to the store
- I scream inside **when** I see bad punctuation.
  - Independent clause:  I scream inside
  - Dependent clause:    when I see bad punctuation

Subordination:

A subordinating conjunction joins and subordinates a clause to an independent clause. The subordinated clause shows its ideas or details are less important than those in the independent clause. Subordination often shows cause, condition, purpose, size, location, details of time, and so on.

By contrast, a coordinating conjunction (and, but, or) joins related independent clauses (see G7). The ideas or details in the coordinated clauses have equal importance.

## G7. Coordinating Conjunctions

Seven coordinating conjunctions join words, phrases, or clauses of the same kind: word to word, phrase to phrase, or clause to clause. They spell the acronym FANBOYS.

|  |  |
|------|-----|
| for | but |
| and | or |
| nor | yet |
|  | so |

- For three days, I ate only <u>bread</u> **and** <u>water</u>.  (words)
- The question is, <u>To be</u> **or** <u>not to be</u>.  (phrases)
- <u>I went shopping</u>, **but** <u>the stores were closed</u>.  (clauses)


## G8. Conjunctive Adverbs and Transitional Expressions

Conjunctive adverbs and transitional expressions join and show the relationship between independent clauses.

Common Conjunctive Adverbs and Transitional Expressions:

| | | |
|---|---|---|
| accordingly | in other words | plus |
| afterward | in summary | presently |
| also | indeed | presumably |
| although | instead | primarily |
| as a result | last | rather |
| at that time | likewise | regardless |
| besides | meanwhile | **second** |
| certainly | more important | similarly |
| consequently | moreover | **so** |
| finally | needless to say | still |
| **first** | nevertheless | that is |
| **for example** | **next** | **then** |
| further | nonetheless | thereafter |
| furthermore | notwithstanding | **therefore** |
| generally | **now** | **thus** |
| hence | obviously | to illustrate |
| **however** | on the contrary | ultimately |
| in addition | on the other hand | usually |
| in comparison | originally | yet |
| in conclusion | otherwise | |
| in contrast | perhaps | |

- I arrived early for the test; **however**, I forgot a pencil.
- Tony joined the meeting late. **Nevertheless**, he beat the boss by 30 seconds.

## G9. Parenthetical Expressions

A parenthetical expression is a comment or explanation expressing an opinion or attitude. It could be removed from the sentence without affecting the meaning.

Common Parenthetical Expressions:

| | | |
|---|---|---|
| apparently | obviously | to be honest |
| as I see it | **of course** | to tell the truth |
| **in fact** | **oh** | **unfortunately** |
| in my opinion | personally | **well** |
| **no** | sitting here today | **yes** |

- **Unfortunately**, I do not recall.
- Mary has an excellent memory. **In fact**, she still remembers her first cell phone number.

## G10. Prepositional Phrases

A preposition connects a noun or pronoun to another word or sentence element. A prepositional phrase begins with a preposition, and it functions as an adverb or adjective.

Common Prepositions:

| | | | |
|---|---|---|---|
| **about** | behind | **in** | outside |
| above | below | in addition to | **over** |
| across | beneath | inside | **through** |
| **after** | beside | instead of | throughout |
| against | between | **into** | **to** |
| along | beyond | near | toward |
| among | **by** | next to | under |
| **around** | **down** | **of** | underneath |
| as | during | **off** | **up** |
| at | except | **on** | upon |
| **because** | except for | onto | **with** |
| **before** | **for** | on top of | within |
| | **from** | **out** | without |

- The book **on the table** is worth $100.
- He ran **around the corner**.

## G11. Verbal Phrases

A verbal phrase begins with a *–ing*, *–ed*, or *to* plus an infinitive verb (shopping, shopped, to shop). It functions as a noun, adverb, or adjective.

- **Shopping for clothes** is relaxing after a long day.
- **Determined to pass the RPR skills test**, the student planned many hours of practice.
- Anthony designs all city parks **to ensure the efficient use of space**.

To test for a verbal phrase, change the sentence tense from present to past or from past to present. If the verb tense for the phrase does <u>not</u> need to be changed, it is a verbal phrase.

Example:
*Shopping for clothes* is relaxing after a long day.

- <u>Test</u>: Change the sentence to past tense.
    - *Shopping for clothes* was relaxing after a long day.
- <u>Result</u>: No change needed for *shopping for clothes*. Therefore, it is a verbal phrase.

## G12. Essential Element

An essential element is a word, phrase, or clause needed for the meaning of the sentence. It defines or restricts the meaning of the sentence element it describes. **Never separate an essential element with punctuation**.

- My cousin **who arrived from Idaho** is visiting me through the weekend.
    - The clause defines which cousin.

- I got the flu **before I was involved in the car accident**.
    - The clause limits *I got the flu*. It defines which flu.

## G13. Nonessential Element

A nonessential element is a word, phrase, or clause <u>not</u> needed for the meaning of the sentence. It only adds information and could be removed without affecting the meaning of the sentence. The thing the nonessential element describes is already defined or restricted. **Always separate a nonessential element with punctuation**.

Sometimes the distinction between an essential and nonessential element is insignificant or difficult to determine.

- Mary, **who is my cousin from Idaho**, is visiting me through the weekend.
  - The relative clause only adds information because Mary is probably known from the context.

- I lost my job last Tuesday, **before I was involved in a car accident**.
  - The dependent clause only adds information. It does not define *last Tuesday*. See G31.

<u>Test for Nonessential Element</u>:
To test for a nonessential element, remove it from the sentence. Did the meaning of the sentence change? If the meaning did not change, the element is nonessential. If it did change, the element is essential.

- Kathy, **in my English class**, is from Germany.
  - The phrase only adds information because the meaning of the sentence (Kathy is from Germany) did not change when "in my English class" was removed. This assumes Kathy is known from the context. Therefore, the element is nonessential, and it is separated with punctuation.

- The students **in my English class** are from China.
  - The phrase is essential because without it the meaning of the sentence changes. The sentence without "in my English class" is about all students, not just the English class students. Therefore, the element is essential, and it is not separated with punctuation.

# Punctuation Overview

## G14. The Period
A period ends a sentence of a statement or command.

English has four sentence types based on structure:
- Simple (G26)
- Compound (G28)
- Complex (G31)
- Compound-Complex (G32)

## G15. The Exclamation Mark
The exclamation mark is <u>not</u> used in court reporting; use a period instead.

In general writing, the exclamation mark should be used sparingly, and it ends a sentence of a strong command or strong statement.

## G16. The Question Mark
A question mark ends a sentence that asks a direct question.

## G17. The Comma
A comma is a general separator. In general writing, the comma is considered a neutral separator compared to the dash (emphasis) and parentheses (de-emphasis).

A comma separates:
- <u>Sentence Elements of the Same Type</u>: coordinate adjectives, items in a series, and independent clauses separated with a coordinating conjunction.

- <u>Sentence Elements of Different Types</u>: parts of a date or address; a direct quotation, introductory element, or nonessential element from the rest of the sentence, and so on.

When an item in a series already contains a comma, use semicolons to separate the items (Rule 43). When a nonessential element already contains a comma, use a dash (preferred) or parentheses to separate the nonessential element (see Rule 58 and Rule 122).

## G18. The Semicolon

A semicolon could be considered a weak period or a strong comma. It predominantly separates sentence elements of the same type.

- Independent clauses separated without a coordinating conjunction.
- Independent clauses in a compound sentence with internal commas where a misreading is likely.
- Items in a series containing internal commas.

## G19. The Colon

A colon generally separates sentence elements of different types. Most often an independent clause from a series, appositive, or explanation.

**An independent clause always precedes a colon.**

## G20. The Hyphen

The hyphen has several uses. Primarily, it joins the words in a compound adjective (ten-story building), It also joins some prefixes and suffixes (ex-husband, pre-1990), and it separates letters in a spelled-out word (S-m-i-t-h).

## G21. The Dash

While both the en dash (–) and em dash (—) punctuate sentences, the em dash is commonly called a "dash" (see Rule 52 about writing an en dash or em dash).

A dash (em dash) is commonly used to separate
- a sudden shift in thought.
- an afterthought at the end of a sentence.
- speaker interruption.
- a nonessential element with internal commas.
- an introductory series from the main clause.

The en dash is mainly used to show a number range (pages 137–142; the years 2013–2017).

## G22. Quotation Marks

Double quotation marks are used

- to indicate a direct quotation from a person or document.
- to emphasize a word or phrase that has unusual or technical usage.
- to indicate the title of a work is contained within a larger work, like a book chapter or magazine article. (Italicize the title of a book, magazine, or newspaper.)
- to indicate the translation or definition of a word or phrase.

## G23. Parentheses

In court reporting, parentheses show explanatory information (exhibits, recess) or indicate witness gestures. They may also separate a nonessential element containing internal commas when dashes would be confusing.

In general writing, parentheses may separate an element not grammatically related to the sentence.

## G24 Brackets

In court reporting, brackets show a change or comment within a direct quotation or indicate a word is written phonetically.

## G25 The Apostrophe

The apostrophe forms a possessive; shows the plural of a lowercase letter; shows the omission of letters in a word or figures in a number; and helps create the verb form of a letter, number, or abbreviation.

# Sentence Types

## G26. Simple Sentence

A simple sentence consists of one independent clause and no dependent clauses (see G4 and G5). While a sentence may begin with a coordinating conjunction, usually *and* or *but*, it should be avoided.

- She kicked the ball.
- I gave him money for a loan.
- And Kendall arrived five minutes early.

## G27. Fragment

A fragment is an elliptical clause that represents a complete clause. Any missing element is understood from the context (see G3). Fragments are common in court reporting, and they are punctuated like a complete clause (Rule 2 to Rule 4).

- MR. SMITH: **Objection. Compound and vague**.
  - These fragments could represent the complete clauses: "I have an objection. The question is compound and vague."

- Q   Where do you work?
  A   **Smith's Auto Repair**.
  - The fragment could represent the complete clause: "I work at Smith's Auto Repair."

## G28. Compound Sentence

A compound sentence consists of two or more independent clauses and no dependent clauses (see G4 and G5). For reading comprehension, the best practice is to limit most compound sentences to only two independent clauses.

Two independent clauses may be separated in the following three ways. The examples use the clauses  "I went to the grocery store" (or "I went to the grocery store and bought eggs, milk, and bread") and "I saw a friend from high school").

1.  A comma with coordinating conjunction.
    If either independent clause contains a comma, consider using a semicolon between the clauses (see Rule 41).
    - I went to the grocery store, **and** I saw a friend from high school.
    - I went to the grocery store and bought eggs, milk, and bread; **and** I saw a friend from high school.

2.  A semicolon without a coordinating conjunction.
    The independent clauses should be closely related (see Rule 39). If they are not closely related, separate the independent clauses with a period.
    - I went to the grocery store; I saw a friend from high school.
      - Or:  grocery store. I saw

3.  A semicolon, a conjunctive adverb (or transitional expression), and a comma.
    Do not place a comma after the conjunctive adverbs *hence, then, thus, so,* or *yet* (Rule 8). A period may be used instead of a semicolon.
    - I went to the grocery store; **consequently,** I saw a friend from high school.
      - Or:  grocery store. **Consequently,** I saw
    - I went to the grocery store; **thus** I saw a friend from high school.
      - Or:  grocery store. **Thus** I saw

Separating three or more independent clauses in a single sentence is the same as separating a series of three or more items (see Rule 13 and Rule 16).


**G29. Compound Predicate**
Do not confuse a compound sentence with a simple sentence containing a compound predicate. A compound sentence has two subjects and two predicates. A simple sentence with a compound predicate has one subject that shares two predicates.

- Lucas visited Brazil and stayed with family
  - The two predicates, "visited Brazil" and "stayed with family," share one subject: *Lucas.*

- I went to the grocery store and saw an old friend from high school.
  - The two predicates, "went to the grocery store" and "saw an old friend from high school," share one subject: *I*

Do <u>not</u> separate the compound predicate with a comma unless it prevents a misreading.

- Maria noticed the real murderer who entered the courtroom, and gasped.
  - The comma clarifies Maria gasped, not the murder.

- Jonathan grabbed the backpack and binders, and dashed out the door.
  - What each *and* joins might be confusing. The comma separates each part of the compound predicate.


## G30. Comma Splice and Run-On Sentence

A **comma splice** occurs when only a comma separates two independent clauses. The coordinating conjunction is missing.

- Our teacher graded the homework, several students received perfect scores.

A **run-on sentence** occurs when two independent clauses have no punctuation between them.

- Our teacher graded the homework several students received perfect scores.

The above comma splice and run-on sentence examples may be correctly punctuated in the following two ways:

- Separated with a period into two sentences.
  - Our teacher graded the homework. Several students received perfect scores.

- Separated with a semicolon if the sentences are closely related (see Rule 39).
  - Our teacher graded the homework; several students received perfect scores.

**G31. Complex Sentence**
A complex sentence consists of one independent clause and one or more dependent clauses (see G4 and G5). A dependent clause may be joined to an independent clause in one of three ways (dependent clause in bold):

1. *Independent clause followed by an essential dependent clause.* No punctuation separates the clauses.

    - I broke my thumb **before I took my summer vacation in Hawaii**.

2. *Independent clause, comma, nonessential dependent clause.* Sometimes the difference between an essential and nonessential dependent clause is insignificant or difficult to determine (see G12 and G13). In those cases, the best practice is to assume the dependent clause is essential.

    - I broke my thumb in January, **before I took my summer vacation in Hawaii**.

3. *Dependent clause, comma, independent clause.*

    - **Before I took my summer vacation in Hawaii**, I broke my thumb.


**G32. Compound-Complex Sentence**
A compound-complex sentence consists of two or more independent clauses and one or more dependent clauses (see G4 and G5). The rules for combining them are the same as those for compound sentences and complex sentences (G28 and G31). If either independent clause contains a comma, consider using a semicolon between the independent clauses (see Rule 41). Dependent clauses are in bold.

- I broke my thumb **before I took my summer vacation in Hawaii**, and the doctor said to use a glove **if I snorkel more than two hours**.

- **Before I took my summer vacation in Hawaii**, I broke my thumb, and the doctor said to use a glove **if I snorkel more than two hours**.
    o Acceptable: my thumb; and the

- Mary, **who is my cousin from Idaho**, is visiting this weekend; and I hope she is not allergic to cats.

# Punctuation Rules

## The Period

### Rule 1. Statement or Command
Use a period to end a statement or command.

Statement:
- The suspect has an alibi.
- I never drive above the speed limit.

Command:
- Can you please state and spell your full name.
- Please speak louder.
  - See Rule 31 for using a comma with *please*.

Use one space after a period (Rule 126).


### Rule 2. Fragment
Use a period after a fragment that represents a complete statement or command (see G27).

Fragments are common in questions, answers, and objections. Punctuated them like a complete statement or command.

- Q   Where do you work, Mr. Smith?
  A   **Bob's Auto Repair**.
  Q   How long have you worked there?
  A   **Five years**.
  Q   **Five years**. Do you work as a mechanic?
  A   Yes. I was an apprentice, but now I'm certified.
  Q   Did you work before that as a certified mechanic?
  A   **At Expert Automotive for a few months**.

See Rule 28 for using a comma or period with *yes* and *no*.

A new topic may appear as a fragment at the beginning of a question. Using a dash might also be appropriate (Rule 53).

- Q   The Honda. Are you the registered owner?
- Q   The group you're in. When do they meet?
  - Or:  you're in—when do

## Rule 3. Fragment in an Objection

Use a period after *objection*, *I object*, or something similar. If the reason following an objection is a fragment, punctuated it like a complete statement. Punctuate a list of reasons like a series of items (see Rule 13 and Rule 16).

- MS. CLARK: Objection. Compound. Objection. Vague.
- MS. CLARK: Objection. Vague. Compound.
- MS. CLARK: Objection. Vague and Compound.
- MS. CLARK: Objection. Beyond the scope, vague, and hearsay.
- MS. CLARK: I object. Facts not in evidence.


## Rule 4. Transitional Fragment or Strong Interjection

At the beginning of a sentence, use a period after a transitional fragment (like *okay, all right, very well,* or *fine*) or after a strong interjection (like *crap, fuck,* or *shit*).

The fragments *okay, all right, very well,* and *fine* are frequently used as a transitional phrase. Other transitional fragments (like *good, great, indeed,* and *of course*) should also be followed with a period. When two or more transitional fragments occur back to back, place a period after each one.

- Q  All right. Fine. What time did you leave?
  A  Shit. I don't recall.
  Q  Very well. Can you tell me if it was morning, afternoon, or evening?
  A  Okay. Great. I think it was early afternoon.

See Rule 29 for using a comma after a mild interjection.


## Rule 5. Polite Request

Use a period after a polite request phrased as a question.

A polite request requires action, not an answer. The words *may* and *will* often begin a polite request.

- Will you mark the exhibit as 5-C.
- May I have a copy of the new exhibit.

# The Comma

**Rule 6. Introductory Subordinate Clause or Verbal Phrase**
Use a comma to separate an introductory subordinate clause or an introductory verbal phrase from an independent clause.

<u>Subordinate Clause</u>:
- Before I left for vacation, I broke my thumb.
- If you finish early, you should start on the next case.

When two or more back-to-back subordinate clauses describe the following independent clause, only use a comma before the independent clause.
- Before I left for vacation but after I took the RPR skills test, I broke my thumb.

<u>Verbal Phrase</u>:
- Determined to pass the RPR skills test, the student planned many hours of practice.
- Shopping for clothes during lunch, I ran into my previous boss.

**Rule 7. Introductory Prepositional Phrase**
Use a comma to separate an introductory prepositional phrase from an independent clause. The comma <u>may</u> be omitted for a two-word phrase that does not reduce clarity.

Comma Required:
- In the late evening, Mr. Smith got $60 from the ATM.
- Upon reaching California, Nancy stopped for lunch.
- Behind the low brick wall, a dog slept in the shade.

Comma May Be Omitted:
- In 1884 tornado deaths dropped by 5 percent.
  - o  Or: In 1884, tornado deaths
- After lunch we saw Ms. Clark at the gas station.
  - o  Or: After lunch, we saw

Comma Needed for Clarity:
- In May, April will graduate from college.
- In 1844, 142 people died in wagon accidents.
  - o  See Rule 185 for a comma with adjacent numbers.

## Rule 8. Introductory Conjunctive Adverb, Transitional Expression, or Parenthetical Expression

Use a comma to separate an introductory conjunctive adverb, introductory transitional expression, or introductory parenthetical expression from an independent clause. Do <u>not</u> place a comma after the conjunctive adverbs *hence, then, thus, so*, or *yet*.

<u>Conjunctive Adverb or Transitional Expression</u>:
In the below examples, a semicolon may separate the two independent clauses (see Rule 42).

- I took the medicine. **Therefore,** I fell asleep quickly.
- I took the medicine. **As a result,** I fell asleep quickly.
- I heard the scream. **However,** I did not call the police.
- I heard the scream. **Thus** I called the police.

<u>Parenthetical Expression</u>:
- **In my opinion,** he stole the jewelry.
- Rose still remembers the license plate number after 20 years. **Obviously,** she has an excellent memory.

## Rule 9. Independent Clauses Joined With a Conjunction

Use a comma to separate two independent clauses joined with a coordinating conjunction. If the clauses are short (four or fewer words each), the comma <u>may</u> be omitted.

- I went to the grocery store, and I saw an old friend from high school.
- The accident investigation starts on page 21, but the analysis of the cause does not begin until page 104.
- I was feeling ill and my friend left.
  - Or:  feeling ill, and my

When there is no coordinating conjunction between the independent clauses, use a period or semicolon (see Rule 39).

When the independent clauses are 17 or more words each, a semicolon may separate the clauses (see Rule 40).

Use a comma to separate smoothly connected clauses joined by the conjunctive adverb *so* or *yet* (see Rule 42).

See G29 for using a comma to separate a compound predicate to prevent a misreading.

**Rule 10. Initial or Concluding Elliptical Clause**
Use a comma to separate an initial or concluding elliptical clause (that stands for a grammatically complete independent or subordinate clause) from another independent clause. A period <u>might</u> also be acceptable (see G26 and Rule 2).

Independent Clause:
- **The receptionist**, and I called the phone number.
  - Complete clause: "I got it from the receptionist."
  - Acceptable:  The receptionist. And I
- **Now and then**, but I have not fully recovered.
  - Complete clause: "I go out now and then."
  - Acceptable:  Now and then. But I
- We looked for the missing child at the elementary school, **at the park**.
  - Complete clause: "and we looked at the park."
- Andrew saw the crime, **yet did not call the police**.
  - Complete clause: "and yet he did not call the police."

Subordinate Clause:
- **If so**, I will bring the document tomorrow.
  - Complete clause: "If that is so."
- **Running late**, call me.
  - Complete clause: "If you are running late."


**Rule 11. Introductory Clause or Phrase Before a Second Independent Clause**
When an introductory phrase or clause precedes the second independent clause in a compound sentence, use a comma before the coordinating conjunction in most cases (see below) and a comma after the introductory phrase or clause. Omit the comma after a one-word conjunctive adverb.

Use a comma before the coordinating conjunction in most cases, but use a semicolon when a misreading is likely (see Rule 41). A misreading is more likely when

- both independent clauses contain at least one internal comma.
- the introductory element or an independent clause contains multiple internal commas.

Use a Comma:
* We can meet Wednesday afternoon, or **if you prefer**, we can meet Thursday morning.
* I arrived late to work, and **when no one was looking**, I snuck into my office.
* Jim spilled coffee on his shirt, and **realizing the boss noticed**, he excused himself.
* Management promoted Tiffany last week, and **to tell you the truth**, everyone was relieved it was not Jacob.

One-Word Conjunctive Adverb (Omit Comma):
* I arrived late to work, and **unfortunately** almost everyone noticed.
* We can meet Wednesday afternoon, or **otherwise** we can meet Thursday morning.

Use a Semicolon:
See Rule 41 for more examples of a semicolon between two independent clauses joined by a coordinating conjunction.

* The office supply shipment lacked the ordered items; and **when I called customer service to return the pens, binders, and paper clips**, they had no record of the order.
* Sarah discussed Tom's unprofessional conduct with the manager; and **if the situation was not corrected with an email, letter, or meeting**, Sarah would contact the union.
* Management, after a quick phone meeting with HR, met with Tom; and **understanding Sarah's concerns**, Tom realized how to communicate better.

### Rule 12. Introductory Dependent Clause Applies to Following Independent Clauses

When an introductory dependent clause applies to both of the following independent clauses, use a comma after the introductory dependent clause and do <u>not</u> use a comma to separate the independent clauses.

Using a comma to separate the independent clauses would indicate the introductory dependent clause applies only to the first independent clause.

- After my spouse called, I immediately left work and I headed straight to the hospital.
  - Not: left work, and I
- Contrary to the rumors, Cody never called Emily and she stayed home that evening.
  - Not: called Emily, and she
- To ensure you are not late for your first work assignment, I recommend setting an extra reminder and Julia recommends arriving 45 minutes early.
  - Not: extra reminder, and Julia


**Rule 13. Series of Items**
Use commas to separate a series of three or more words, phrases, or clauses. Use a comma before the final item.

The serial or "Oxford" comma is the comma before the coordinating conjunction (*and, or, nor*) of the final item. While a serial comma is technically not required, most style guides highly recommend or require its use. Court reporting requires the serial comma to avoid ambiguity.

Because a person may omit the coordinating conjunction before the final item when speaking, the court reporting rule is to use commas to separate a series of three or more words, phrases, or clauses (see second and fourth examples).

- The training included John, Mary, Bob, and Barbara.
- The training included John, Mary, Bob, Barbara.

- I bought milk, bread, and eggs.
- I bought milk, bread, eggs.

- Josephine said she would never live near the ocean, by a lake, or even next to a pond.

- Randy moved to New York, Frank relocated to San Francisco, and Susan stayed in Chicago.

See Rule 43 when a series contains internal commas.

See Rule 44 when a series consists of long dependent clauses.

See Rule 59 when a series begins a sentence.

## Rule 14. Comma After *Et Cetera* or a Series of Items

Only use a comma after *et cetera* or a series of items when another punctuation rule requires it.

*The Chicago Manual of Style* does not require a comma after *et cetera* and considers the practice "traditional usage." However, *The Gregg Reference Manual* requires a comma after *et cetera*. Do <u>not</u> abbreviate *et cetera* (Rule 193).

- The instructor invited John, Mary, Bob, and Barbara to the employee training.
- My son grabbed his swimsuit, beach towel, et cetera for a trip to the beach.
  - *Gregg*: beach towel, et cetera, for a trip
- Seeing John, Mary, Bob, and Barbara, the instructor greeted them warmly.
  - Comma after series required per Rule 6.
- When my son grabbed his swimsuit, beach towel, et cetera, he forgot his cell phone.
  - Comma after *et cetera* required per Rule 6.

## Rule 15. Comma Before Ampersand

Do <u>not</u> use a comma before an ampersand (&) in a series of three or more items. However, a comma before an ampersand might occur in a business or organization name. Follow the preference or official spelling of the business or organization.

- Do you have the telephone number for Ms. Rivas of Adams, Rivas & Smith?
- The conference rooms are very small at Dewey, Cheetham & Howe.
- The deposition for the Kramer case is Tuesday morning at Coleman, Orrick, & Weintraub
  - The firm's official name contains a comma.

## Rule 16. Series of Items Connected With Conjunctions

When all the items in a series are connected with coordinating conjunctions (*and, or, nor*), do <u>not</u> use commas to separate the items.

When a person omits an *and* between two items while speaking, place a comma for the missing *and* for clarity (see second and fifth examples).

- I bought bread and milk.
- I bought bread, milk.
- I bought bread and milk and eggs.

- The training included John and Mary and Bob and Barbara.
- The training included John and Mary, Bob and Barbara.

- Josephine said she would never live near the ocean or by a lake or even next to a pond.


## Rule 17. Nonessential Clause or Phrase

Use a comma (end of sentence) or commas (midsentence) to separate a nonessential subordinate clause, verbal phrase, prepositional phrase, transitional expression, or parenthetical expression.

Always separate a nonessential element with punctuation, and never separate an essential element with punctuation (G12 and G13). Some midsentence examples may also be seen as interrupting the sentence flow, which requires a comma for separation (Rule 18).

Subordinate Clause:
- Pharmco's principal office, **which is in Ohio**, has an excellent reputation.
- Keith moved to New York in 2013, **when he was 23**.
  - Acceptable:  in 2013 when he  (see G31)

Verbal Phrase:
- The 2016 document, **written before Tom's death**, states his soon-to-be ex-wife borrowed the money.

- Sandra applied to Stanford University this year, **graduating high school last May**.
  - See Rule 19.
- They evicted Tim, **having failed to collect any rent**.
  - See Rule 19.

Prepositional Phrase:
- Linda's condition, **on the whole**, is improving.
- Linda's condition is improving, **on the whole**.

Transitional or Parenthetical Expression:
- I studied hard for the exam. The results, **however**, showed not hard enough.
- I rather not attend the party, **to tell you the truth**.

## Rule 18. Interrupting Word, Phrase, or Clause

Use commas to separate a word, phrase, or clause that interrupts the flow of the sentence.

The interrupting word, phrase, or clause often comes between the subject and the verb.

- The injured victim, **because of blood loss**, collapsed.
- Mr. Smith, **exactly 16 minutes after the meeting**, called with the information I requested.
- Ms. Anderson is being sued, **so I have been told**, by her previous attorney.
- It happened, **you know**, in the middle of dinner.
- I, **like**, worry, **like**, all the time.

## Rule 19. Participle Phrase at the End of a Sentence

When a participle phrase at the end of a sentence is nonessential, separate it with a comma. When the phrase is essential, do <u>not</u> separate it with a comma. (See G12 and G13.)

A participle phrase (verbal phrase typically starting with a word ending in *-ing* or *-ed*) is usually essential when it directly follows the word it describes. It is usually nonessential when it describes an earlier word (often the subject) in the sentence.

- Do I dare pet the big dog **licking its lips**?
- Gabriel saw his father **walking along the shoreline**.
- I called the phone number to get customer service, **needing to connect to a video call in 30 minutes**.
- The bank put the certificate into a safe deposit box, **wanting to protect it**.
- The home was never rebuilt, **destroyed by fire**.
- The cruel scheme was the landlord's downfall, **calculated to remove the elderly tenants**.

## Rule 20. Nominative Absolute

Use a comma (beginning or end of sentence) or commas (midsentence) to separate a nominative absolute.

A nominative absolute is a noun or pronoun followed by a modifier, usually a participle phrase (see Rule 19 description). The nominative absolute modifies (describes) the sentence, but it is not grammatically related to it.

- **The soldiers needing help**, reinforcements soon arrived.
- **The carpets now clean**, we moved the furniture back into the living room.
- They said their final goodbye, **the truck fully loaded**, and drove away.
- The knight sheathed his sword, **the dragon finally slain**.
- I sat anxiously next to another bus passenger, **our legs touching**.

## Rule 21. Contrasting Phrase

Use a comma (end of sentence) or commas (midsentence) to separate a contrasting phrase.

Word or phrases beginning a contrasting phrase include *but, even though, never, not, rather, rather than,* and *though*. Do <u>not</u> separate a contrasting phrase beginning with the word *and* (*and but, and never*).

The comma <u>may</u> be omitted if the contrasting phrase, usually a *but* phrase, does not interrupt the sentence flow.

- Plead for mercy, **not justice**.
- The staff meeting occurs on Mondays, **never Tuesdays**.
- They traveled to Chicago on Monday, **rather than Tuesday**, as the report indicates.
- I said Jack **and never Jill** drove the getaway car.
- Diana's vacation was short **but enjoyable**.

## Rule 22. Direct Address

Use a comma (beginning or end of sentence) or commas (midsentence) to separate a name, title, or words used as direct address.

Beginning of the Sentence:
- **Mr. Smith**, please email the document.
- **Angela**, did you have lunch with your friends?
- **Ladies and gentlemen**, we will now break for lunch.

Midsentence:
- Please tell us, **Ms. Anderson**, where you work.
- With all due respect, **Captain**, I disagree.
  - See Rule 142 for capitalization of titles.

End of the Sentence:
- I called in sick that day, **Michelle**.
- Can I count on your support, **sir**?
  - Do <u>not</u> capitalize *sir*, *ma'am*, or *miss* (Rule 142).

## Rule 23. Coordinate Adjectives

Use a comma to separate two adjectives that equally modify (describe) the following noun.

- She bought a **sleek, shiny** car.
- He has been a **faithful, sincere** friend.

Adjectives that equally modify the following noun are called coordinate adjectives. They describe the same "quality":
- Opinion (good, beautiful)
- Size (round, square)
- Age (old, new)
- Color (red, blue)
- Origin (American, German)
- Material (wood, stone)

Coordinate adjectives can answer *yes* to the following tests:
1.  Can "and" be inserted sensibly between the adjectives?
2.  Can the adjectives be sensibly reversed?

Example 1: She bought a **sleek, shiny** car.
- Test 1: She bought a sleek and shiny car.    (Yes)
- Test 2: She bought a shiny, sleek car.        (Yes)
- Result: *shiny* and *sleek* are coordinate adjectives.

Example 2: He has been a **faithful, sincere** friend.
- Test 1: He has been a faithful and sincere friend.  (Yes)
- Test 2: He has been a sincere, faithful friend.      (Yes)
- Result: *faithful* and *sincere* are coordinate adjectives.

When three or more coordinate adjectives precede a noun, use a comma between the adjectives. Do <u>not</u> place a comma between the final adjective and the noun. Use Rule 13 as a guideline.

- Did the witness speak in a **relaxed, confident, controlled** manner?
- The **older, skilled, resourceful** worker always arrived 15 minutes before work.

Cumulative Adjectives:
When adjectives are not coordinate adjectives, they are cumulative adjectives because each adjective describes a different quality. Do <u>not</u> separate cumulative adjectives with a comma.

- We saw an **old black** bear.
  - *Old* is an opinion; *black* regards species or color.

- We ate **German chocolate** cake.
  - *German* regards origin; *chocolate* is a material.

- We bought two **round wooden** tables.
  - *Round* is a shape; *wooden* is a material.

See Rule 109 for identifying a compound adjective.

**Rule 24. Title and Degree After a Person's Name**
Use commas to separate a title or degree after a person's name.

- Ruth Walker, **CEO**, approved the revised budget.
- We spoke to Mr. Smith, **PhD**, for more information.
- Ms. Anderson, **Esq.**, will represent Mr. Smith in the criminal case.

See Rule 141 for a title after a person's name.

See Rule 160 for capitalizing a degree after a person's name.

See Rule 194 for not using periods in an abbreviation of a title or degree after a person's name.

**Rule 25. Jr. and Sr. With a Person's Name**
Do <u>not</u> use commas to separate *Jr.* or *Sr.* with a person's name unless a person prefers it. Never use commas to separate a numerical designation with a person's name.

- Robert Smith **Sr.** graduated high school in 1956.
- Robert Smith **Jr.** graduated high school in 1982.
- Robert Smith, **Jr.**, graduated high school in 1982.
  - Person prefers commas.
- Robert Smith **III** graduated high school in 2011.

**Rule 26. Appositive Adjective and Nonessential Appositive**
Use a comma (end of sentence) or commas (midsentence) to separate an appositive adjective or nonessential appositive.

An appositive adjective is an adjective that follows the noun. An appositive is a noun or phrase that renames a preceding noun or pronoun.

Always separate a nonessential element with punctuation, and never separate an essential element with punctuation (G12 and G13).

To help distinguish an essential appositive from a nonessential appositive, note the location of the proper noun (see Rule 137). When an appositive follows a proper noun, the appositive is usually nonessential. When a proper noun is the appositive, the appositive is typically essential.

Nonessential Appositive:
- Dr. Cooper, **my psychologist**, last saw me in June.
- Bizen ware, **a dark stoneware**, was produced in Japan for centuries.
- High-speed roadways, **especially freeways**, have higher accident rates.
- My youngest brother, **Jack**, is an attorney.

Essential Appositive:
- My sister **Jane** is an attorney.
  - If the person has only one sister, the appositive is nonessential and should be separated with commas (My sister, Jane, is an attorney).
- Was the resident **Mr. Smith** home at the time?
  - If there is only one resident, the appositive is nonessential and should be separated with commas (Was the resident, Mr. Smith, home at the time?).

Appositive Adjective:
- Jim was a big boy, **tall and strong**.
- I love steak, **lean and tender**, served with a Caesar salad.

Phrase Regarding Residence of Business Connection:
Use commas to separate a long phrase of six or more words that specifies a person's residence or business connection. Do not use commas for a short phrase. This type of phrase usually begins with the word *of*.

- Officer Sanchez, **of the San Jose Police Department**, took several witness statements.
- Dr. Cooper, **of North Dakota WeCare Health Care Group**, is my primary doctor.
- Dr. Cooper **of WeCare Health** is my doctor.
- Ms. Wilcox **of Los Angeles** will arrive next Monday.

**Rule 27. Enumerations**
Use a comma (beginning or end of sentence) or commas (midsentence) to separate a word, number, or letter used for enumeration (*first, second, secondly, lastly, one, two, A, B*).

A series of enumerated items is often separated with semicolons because words have been omitted (Rule 35), the clauses are closely related (Rule 39), or the series of items contains internal commas (Rule 43).

- **First**, I want to thank Allison. **Second**, I want to give her a small gift.
- I wanted a roommate, **first**, for financial support; **secondly**, for safety.
- There is, **lastly**, no evidence for the accusation.
- We need the following: **one**, an application; **two**, a driver's license; and, **three**, a birth certificate.
  - See Rule 46.

See Rule 46 for enumerated phrases.


## Rule 28. The Words *Yes* and *No*

Use a comma to separate *yes* or *no* when it is used as a parenthetical expression. However, use a period to separate *yes* or *no* when it is used as a fragment.

When *yes* or *no* can be removed without affecting the meaning of the sentence, use a comma because it is being used as a parenthetical expression (see G9). In this case, *yes* or *no* is usually echoing a statement or question.

When *yes* or *no* is accompanied with additional or explanatory information, use a period because it is most likely being used as a fragment (see G27).

Parenthetical Expression:
- Q  Do you work for the San Jose Police Department?
  A  Yes, I do.
- Q  Did you see the suspect leave the office that day?
  A  I didn't see her leave, no.

Fragment:
- Q  Do you work for the San Jose Police Department?
  A  Yes.  Six years under Captain Lewis.
- Q  Did you see the suspect leave the office that day?
  A  No. I was in a meeting until 6:00 p.m.

**Rule 29. Mild Interjection**
Use a comma to separate a mild interjection.

- Wow, a garter snake just slithered under that log.
- Well, I have no idea how that happened.
- I forgot to pack my toothbrush, shoot.

See Rule 4 for using a period after a strong interjection.


**Rule 30. The Words *Now* and *Then***
When the word *now* or *then* begins a sentence and has the meaning of *well*, separate it with a comma. If *now* or *then* relates to time or sequence, do <u>not</u> separate it with a comma.

- Now, that is a fast motorcycle.
- Now, if you would use the recipe, it will taste better.
- Now is the time to practice.
- Should we go now?
- I was 15 in 1990. Now I feel old.
- Then, all things considered, it was a valiant attempt.
- Sam went to the grocery store. Then he got gas.


**Rule 31. The Word *Please***
Only separate the word *please* with a comma when it occurs at the end of a sentence.

- Please speak louder
- Can you please speak louder
- Can you speak louder, please.
- Please show us where you were sitting.
- Show us please where you were sitting.
- Show us where you were sitting, please.


**Rule 32. The Word *Too***
Only separate the word *too* with commas when it means *also* and comes between the subject and the verb.

- James wanted a bigger piece of the pie too.
- James, too, wanted a bigger piece of the pie.
- You should be in Hawaii too.
- You, too, should be in Hawaii.

## Rule 33. Phrase Starting With *Including, Such As,* or *Like*

Use a comma to separate a nonessential phrase beginning with *including, such as,* or *like*. When the phrase is essential, do <u>not</u> use a comma.

Always separate a nonessential element with punctuation, and never separate an essential element with punctuation (see G12 and G13).

Nonessential Phrase:
- Tammy loves to travel to distant countries, like Spain, China, and Brazil.
- I prepare many engineering documents, such as reports and project plans.
- The kidnap victim suffered many awful things for three weeks, including torture and starvation.
    - Or (if deemed essential):  three weeks including

Essential Phrase:
- Send me a text message including your plans for this holiday weekend.
- Next year Ethan wants to visit a location like the Colosseum or Notre Dame.
- Many trees such as elms and oaks do not grow in this climate.


## Rule 34. *Inc., LLC,* or *Ltd.* in a Business Name

Do <u>not</u> use commas to separate *Inc., LLC, Ltd.,* or a similar term in a business name unless the official spelling of the business name contains it.

When commas are used for separation, do <u>not</u> use a comma after *Inc., LLC, Ltd.,* or a similar term when followed by another punctuation mark or when it is at the end of a sentence.

- The CFO for Insight Sales, Inc., just scheduled a meeting with all accounting staff.
    - The official business name has a comma.
- The CFO of Insight Sales, Inc.—was she there?
- The company in question is Insight Sales, Inc.

- Apple Inc. was founded in 1976 as Apple Computer Company in Los Altos, California.
- Did you sign a contract with Bob's Concrete LLC to redo the driveway?

## Rule 35. Comma to Indicate Missing Words
Use a comma to indicate a missing word or phrase that creates a break in sentence flow.

The missing word or phrase is usually the word *that*, a preposition, or a repetitive word or phrase from the first clause of a compound sentence. A semicolon often separates the clauses because they are closely related (see Rule 39).

- The fact is simply, we're bankrupt.
  - The comma represents a missing "that."
- I volunteer two hours each morning at the animal shelter, Saturday and Sunday.
  - The comma represents a missing "on."
- To error is human; to forgive, divine
  - The comma represents the repetitive word "is."
- For adults the admission fee is $7; for children, $5.
  - The comma represents the repetitive phrase "the admission fee is."

Use a comma between a two-part expression, especially where many words are missing.

- Easy come, easy go.
- Garbage in, garbage out.
- First come, first serve.

## Rule 36. Comma to Prevent a Misreading
Use a comma to prevent a misreading or to add needed clarity. This situation often occurs with repeated words.

- Whoever it **is, is** in big trouble with the main office.
- A **long, long** time ago in a galaxy **far, far** away.
- **Now, now**, you shouldn't expect an A on the test if you did not study.
- Like **Dolly, Madison** collects cat-themed merchandise.

**Rule 37. State or Country Directly Follows City Name**
Use commas to separate a state or country name when it directly follows a city name. See Rule 177 for address formatting.

- Is Mountain Home, Arkansas, in Baxter County?
- I lived in Toyoko, Japan, for three years.
- Headquartered in Cupertino, California, Apple Inc. was founded in 1976 as Apple Computer Company.
- I accidentally booked a flight to Springfield, New Zealand, instead of Springfield, Illinois.

**Rule 38. Commas With Month-Day-Year Formatted Date**
Use a comma after the day in a month-day-year formatted date. Use a comma after the year if the date is midsentence. See Rule 171 for date formatting.

- My son was born on April 5, 2013.
- I went on June 18, 2018, to see the doctor.

# The Semicolon

**Rule 39. Independent Clauses Without a Conjunction**
A semicolon <u>may</u> separate two closely related independent clauses joined without a coordinating conjunction. Using a period to separate the clauses is always acceptable.

The two independent clauses should be closely related by meaning, content, or grammatical structure. Whether or not the clauses are closely related is left for the court reporter to decide. Often the first independent clause creates an expectation, and the second independent clause fulfills it.

- The wallet was not in my purse; my anxiety exploded.
  - Or:  my purse. My anxiety
- The football play caused a large tear in Mark's jersey; he hoped a coach could quickly repair it.
  - Or:  Mark's jersey. He hoped
- The newspaper headline emphasized the dramatic outcome; the article contained the mundane details causing the event.
  - Or:  dramatic outcome. The article

**Rule 40. Long Independent Clauses With a Conjunction**
A semicolon <u>may</u> separate two long independent clauses (each 17 or more words) joined with a coordinating conjunction when a stronger-than-comma break adds clarity. Using a comma to separate the clauses is always acceptable.

A comma normally separates two independent clauses joined with a coordinating conjunction (Rule 9), but a semicolon between two long independent clauses may add clarity to the separation. Because a sentence may begin with a coordinating conjunction, the independent clauses could also be written as separate sentences. This should be avoided (see G26).

- Susan offered to guarantee the very large personal loan for the kitchen remodel with her recently purchased and expensive sports car; but the bank's chief loan officer immediately denied the large personal loan application without even calling or emailing her.
  - Or:  sports car, but the
  - Or (avoid):  sports car. But the

- Many people think they could solve all of society's problems if given complete power over the laws and available resources; but people usually lack a coherent and detailed plan that may be objectively reviewed and evaluated by experts and authorities.
  - Or:  available resources, but people
  - Or (avoid):  available resources. But people

**Rule 41. Joined Independent Clauses With Internal Commas**
Use a semicolon to separate two independent clauses joined with a coordinating conjunction when a misreading is likely due to internal commas.

A misreading is more likely when

- both independent clauses contain at least one internal comma.
- an introductory element or an independent clause contains multiple internal commas.

Using a period to separate the clauses is also acceptable, but should be avoided (see G26). See Rule 11 for more examples.

- I ordered pens, pencils, and paper; and I had them mailed using express delivery.
  - Not: and paper, and I
  - Or (avoid): and paper. And I

- When I came to, I saw the assailant with a knife in their hand; and if I had regained consciousness a few moments later, I would be dead.
  - Not: their hand, and I
  - Or (avoid): their hand. And I

- We can meet Wednesday afternoon; or if you prefer, we can meet Thursday morning, Friday afternoon, or Monday morning.
  - Not: Wednesday afternoon, or if
  - Or (avoid): Wednesday afternoon. Or if


## Rule 42. Independent Clauses With Conjunctive Adverb or Transitional Expression

A semicolon <u>may</u> separate two independent clauses joined with a conjunctive adverb or transitional expression. Using a period to separate the clauses is always acceptable.

Place a comma after the conjunctive adverb or transitional expression. However, do <u>not</u> place a comma after *hence, then, thus, so*, and *yet* (Rule 8).

- I heard the scream; however, I did not call the police.
  - Or: the scream. However, I did

- I heard the scream; thus I called the police.
  - Or: the scream. Thus I called

- I took the medicine; as a result, I fell asleep quickly.
  - Or: the medicine. As a result, I fell

Use a comma to separate two closely related independent clauses that are smoothly connected by the conjunctive adverb *so* or *yet* (see Rule 9 and Rule 39).

- The discounted Halloween decorations were selling fast, so buy them while they last.

**Rule 43. Series of Items With Internal Commas**
Use semicolons to separate a series of three or more phrases
or clauses containing internal commas.

Commas normally separate a series of items (see Rule 13).
However, semicolons are used to separate each item in the
series when at least one item contains a comma.

- I have lived in Cincinnati, Ohio; Seattle, Washington;
  and Santa Cruz, California.

- Mira paid rent of $1,500 on April 2, 2022; $1,500 on
  May 1, 2022; but only $900 on June 16, 2022.

- The attendance figures came at 10:00 p.m.: Zone 1,
  233; Zone 2, 132; Zone 3, 265; and Zone 4, 118.


**Rule 44. Series of Long Dependent Clauses**
Semicolons <u>may</u> separate a series of three or more long
dependent clauses (each 17 or more words). Using commas
to separate the clauses is always acceptable.

Commas normally separate a series of three or more clauses
(see Rule 13). However, semicolons between the long
dependent clauses may add clarity to the separation.

- She is forgetting that Mr. Smith offered to spend several
  days with another attorney to thoroughly go over the files
  and records before the **audit; that** Mr. Smith offered to
  give all the files and records to the attorney three weeks
  prior to **audit; and that** Mr. Smith offered to pay their own
  accountant to assist us in case there were any questions
  or problems.
  - Or: audit, that . . . audit, and that

- If Ms. Anderson had tried some special sales promotion
  and was not able to raise all the necessary **funds; if** she
  had tried to borrow the funds and was not able to find a
  willing **lender; if** she had offered to sell part of the
  declining business and was not been able to find another
  business **partner; then** it seems that the only course of
  action is to close the doors and to go out of business.
  - Or: funds, if . . . lender, if . . . partner, then

## Rule 45. Clause or Phrase at the End of a Sentence Starting With *For Example*, *Namely*, or *That Is*

For most situations, use a semicolon before a clause or phrase at the end of a sentence starting with *for example*, *namely*, or *that is*. A colon, dash, or comma instead of a semicolon <u>may</u> also be appropriate (see below discussion). A comma always follows *for example*, *namely*, or *that is*.

Four situations follow the words *for example*, *namely*, or *that is* (*The Chicago Manual of Style* and *The Gregg Reference Manual* preferences are in parentheses):

- <u>Afterthought</u>. Use a semicolon (*Chicago* and *Gregg*). A dash <u>may</u> be used if the clause or phrase needs emphasis.

- <u>Explanatory or Illustrative Independent Clause</u>. Use a semicolon (*Chicago*) or colon (*Gregg*). A colon is consistent with Rule 47. A dash <u>may</u> be used if the clause or phrase needs emphasis.

- <u>List</u>. Use a semicolon (*Chicago*) or colon (*Gregg*). A colon is consistent with Rule 47. A dash <u>may</u> be used if the clause or phrase needs emphasis.

- <u>Appositive</u>. Use a dash (*Chicago*) or comma (*Gregg*).

Examples:
- <u>Afterthought:</u> The offer lacks a basic title; for example, "Offer to Build a House."
  - o  Or (emphasis):  basic title—for example, "Offer

- <u>Explanatory or Illustrative Clause</u>: The offer lacks one thing; namely, who pays for the removal work.
  - o  Or:  one thing: namely, who
  - o  Or (emphasis):  one thing—namely, who

- <u>List</u>: The offer lacks things; that is, an itemized cost estimate, a schedule, and a contact number.
  - o  Or:  lacks things: that is, an
  - o  Or (emphasis):  lacks things—that is, an

- <u>Appositive</u>: The offer lacks one critical thing—that is, a schedule.
  - o  Or:  critical thing, that is, a

## Rule 46. Enumerated Phrases

Use commas to separate a list of enumerated phrases that are short and contain no internal commas. However, use semicolons to separate a list of enumerated phrases when many phrases are long (12 or more words each) or when at least one phrase contains internal commas.

Depending on what a person says, use a figure or lowercase letter to enumerate each phrase. Enclose the figure or letter beginning each enumerated phrase in parentheses.

<u>Short Phrases Without Internal Commas</u>:
Alternatively, but not preferred, the number may be expressed in words or an uppercase letter used (see Rule 27).

- I was told to eat more (1) apples, (2) pears, and (3) bananas.
    - Acceptable (not preferred): I was told to eat more, one, apples; two, pears; and, three, bananas.
- We need the following: (1) an application, (2) a driver's license, and (3) a birth certificate.
    - Acceptable (not preferred): We need the following: one, an application; two, a driver's license; and, three, a birth certificate.
- Ms. Clark's claim (a) has zero evidence, (b) has no witnesses, and (c) contradicts previous testimony.
    - Acceptable (not preferred): Ms. Clark's claim, A, has zero evidence; B, has no witnesses; and, C, contradicts previous testimony.

<u>Many Long Phrases</u>:
- The manager shall (1) track all inventory in the warehouse at 493 Main Street; (2) maintain the work schedule for all employees at the warehouse in order to have enough staffing for three eight-hour shifts; and (3) hire all temporary warehouse shipping staff and office bookkeeping staff during the holiday rush period.

<u>Internal Commas</u>:
- I have lived in (a) Cincinnati, Ohio; (b) Seattle, Washington; and (c) Santa Cruz, California.
- Tim's teammates are (1) John, a police officer; (2) Tobias, an architect; and (3) Steve, a baker.

# The Colon

## Rule 47. Independent Clause Followed by a List, Appositive, or Explanation

Use a colon to separate an independent clause from a following

- list.
- appositive.
- explanatory independent clause.

**An independent clause always precedes the colon.** However, a word, phrase, list, or clause may follow the colon.

See Rule 45 for a colon with *for example*, *namely*, or *that is*.

See Rule 71 for a colon before a question within a sentence.

See Rule 75 for a colon before a direct quotation.

List:
When an introductory phrase or independent clause contains or ends with the phrase *as follows* or *the following*, always use a colon between the phrase or clause and the list.

- I shipped a box full of books on different topics: math, science, and history.
- The steps are as follows: get an incident number, fill out the form, and mail or email the form.

Appositive:
- I attend only one type of music festival: jazz.
- Junk food has two huge disadvantages: fat and calories.

Explanatory Independent Clause:
A period or semicolon may also be appropriate (see Rule 39).

- The local "laws" are different: you are guilty unless proven innocent.
  - Or: are different; you are
  - Or: are different. You are

- I have two observations about the witness: Brandon has a criminal record and has perjured himself.
  - Or: the witness; Brandon has
  - Or: the witness. Brandon has

## Rule 48. Capitalization After a Colon

Capitalize the first word after a colon when

- the word is a proper noun or adjective (see Rule 137).
- two or more related sentences follow.
  - *The Chicago Manual of Style* and *The Gregg Reference Manual* follow this rule.
  - *The Redbook* allows capitalization when one or more related sentences follow.
  - The *Associated Press Stylebook* capitalizes when one or more related sentences follow.
- one or more sentences follow that need emphasis, such as a statement of a rule or principle.

Examples:

- I have two observations about this witness that will hurt the case: Brandon's previous perjury and criminal record.
- The local "laws" are different: First, you are guilty unless proven innocent. Second, the sheriff is always right.
- George was in a difficult situation: He could lie and escape embarrassment, but he would feel guilty. Or he could tell the uncomfortable truth.
- Here is a fundamental punctuation rule: Always separate a nonessential element with punctuation.


## Rule 49. Colon After Speaker Identification

Use a colon after speaker identification in a transcript.

- MR. SMITH: Where were you at 3:15 p.m.?
- MS. ANDERSON: Objection. Vague.
- THE COURT: Please rephrase your question.


## Rule 50. QUESTION and ANSWER in Readback

Use a colon after the words *QUESTION* and *ANSWER* in transcription readback. Use all capital letters for these words.

- Let me quote your previous testimony.

  "QUESTION: What time did you leave for work?
  "ANSWER: About 7:15 a.m.
  "QUESTION: How certain are you of the time?
  "ANSWER: Within a few minutes."

See Rule 77 for quotation marks with paragraphed material.

### Rule 51. Colon After *Note*, *Caution*, or *Warning*

Use a colon after the words *note*, *caution*, or *warning* when the word introduces instruction or a guideline. Capitalize the first word after the colon.

- Note: All timesheets are due on Fridays by noon.
- A very concerned resident placed a "Caution: Duck Crossing" sign near the pond.
- The sign on the fence states, "Warning: Dogs."

## The Dash

### Rule 52. Typing a Dash

While both the en dash (–) and em dash (—) punctuate sentences, **the em dash is commonly called a "dash"** (see Rule 53 to Rule 62 for using a dash; see Rule 186 for using an en dash to show a page or year range).

Use the en dash character (–) or em dash character (—) without a space on either side of the character. When these characters are not available, use one hyphen (-) for the en dash character and two connected hyphens (--) for the em dash character.

Em Dash Character Available:
- Many things changed this year—mostly for the better.
- We—Tom, Sue, and Bill—formed the legal team for the prominent client.

Em Dash Character Not Available:
- Many things changed this year--mostly for the better.
- We--Tom, Sue, and Bill--formed the legal team for the prominent client.

Traditionally, court reporters wrote an em dash using two connected hyphens with a space before and after (word -- word) because the typewriter had no em dash character and the spaces provided a better visual break.

Do not capitalize the first word after a dash unless it is the word *I,* a proper noun, or a proper adjective (Rule 138).

## Rule 53. Abrupt Break or Afterthought

Use a dash (end of sentence) or dashes (midsentence) to separate an abrupt break in thought. Use a dash to separate an afterthought at the end of a sentence.

Abrupt Break:
- Ethan exited his truck and went—sprinted to the overturned car engulfed in flames.

- Olivia asked me—her husband was away on business—to watch her two young children.
    - See Rule 61 for <u>not</u> using a period after a statement within a sentence separated with dashes.

- Q   The group you're in—when do they meet?
    - Or:  you're in. When do  (see Rule 2).

Afterthought:
- DiMaggio's has the best pizza in town—the fastest delivery too.

- Many things changed this year—mostly for the better.

- My spouse and I traveled along the California coastline—a typical weekend getaway.
    - This afterthought is a sentence summary.


## Rule 54. Speaker Interruption

Use a dash after a speaker is interrupted.

- Q   How old were you when your brother—
  A   Twenty-five.

- Q   Were you home at the time of—
  A   No.

- Q   Is this your signature—
  A   Yes.


Speaker interruption is an example of an abrupt break that requires a dash.

### Rule 55. Speaker Continuation After Interruption

Use a dash before the continuation of a speaker who was interrupted and is continuing their original thought.

- Q   How old were you when your brother—
  A   Twenty-five.
  Q   —tragically passed away?

- Q   Were you home at the time of—
  A   No.
  Q   —the break-in?

When the continuation occurs after a brief statement or fragment, use a dash between the brief statement or fragment and the continuation. Do not use a period before an opening dash (see Rule 60). The continuation may start on a new line to improve readability.

- Q   Is this your signature—
  A   Yes.
  Q   Let me finish—on Check No. 7403?
      Or:
  Q   Let me finish.
      —on Check No. 7403?


### Rule 56. Interrupter Continues Speaker's Thought

No punctuation is preferred before an interrupter who continues another speaker's thought. A dash was traditionally used in court reporting and is acceptable.

- Q   You stated that you saw a speeding red—
  A   Porsche.
    - Or: —Porsche.
  Q   Do you know the model?

- Q   What direction were you driving?
  A   I was going north on Ridge—
  Q   Valley Ridge Way.
    - Or: —Valley Ridge Way.
  A   Yes.

- Q   What direction were you driving?
  A   I was going north on—
  Q   Valley Ridge—
    - Or: —Valley Ridge—
    - Interrupter continues the thought and is interrupted.
  A   Yes—towards Nebraska Street.
    - Thought continuation after "Yes" (Rule 55).

## Rule 57. The Words *Strike That* and *Correction*

Use a dash (end of sentence) or dashes (midsentence) with the words *strike that* or *correction*.

The phrase *strike that* is typically followed by a period because the speaker normally starts a new sentence. The word *correction* usually occurs as a midsentence abrupt break.

- Did you purchase—strike that. What did you do in the store?
- When did—strike that. How did Andrew manage to get your credit card?
- How did Andy—correction—Andrew manage to get your credit card?
- I was traveling Monday night—correction—Tuesday night when the accident occurred.


## Rule 58. Sentence Element With Internal Commas

Use dashes to separate a sentence element that contains internal commas and requires separation with punctuation. The sentence element is often nonessential.

- We—Tom, Sue, and Bill—formed the legal team for the prominent client.
  - Not: We, Tom, Sue, and Bill, formed the
- The witness—reluctant, soft-spoken, and nervous—described a single suspect.
- In major three cities—Chicago, Detroit, and New York—crime decreased last quarter.

Parentheses <u>may</u> be used when dashes could be confusing (usually by being used elsewhere in the sentence) or when parentheses noticeably improve readability (see Rule 122).

- We (Tom from Lee's Law Group; Sue from Carter, Watson & White; and Bill from Murphy and Sons LLP) formed the super—correction—combined legal team for the prominent client who lives in Spokane, Washington.
- In major three cities (Chicago, Illinois; Detroit, Michigan; and New York City, New York), crime decreased last quarter—mostly for the better.

**Rule 59. Series at the Beginning of a Sentence**
Use a dash after a series of items at the beginning of a
sentence.

- Tom, Sue, and Bill—we formed the legal team for the
  prominent client.

- Reluctant, soft-spoken, and nervous—the witness
  described a single suspect.


**Rule 60. Punctuation Before an Opening Dash**
Do <u>not</u> use a period, comma, colon, or semicolon before an
opening dash. However, use a period before an opening dash
when it is part of an abbreviation.

- The information is correct—and you know it.
  - Not:  is correct,—and you
- Q   Is this your signature—
  A   Yes.
  Q   Let me finish—on Check No. 7403?
    - Not:  me finish.—on check
- Things changed by 9:00 p.m.—mostly for the better.


**Rule 61. Statement or Question Separated With Dashes**
**            Within a Sentence**
When a statement or fragment is separated with dashes within
a sentence, do <u>not</u> use a period before the closing dash. When
a long direct question of four or more words is separated with
dashes within a sentence, use a question mark before the
closing dash.

- Olivia asked me—her husband was away on
  business—to watch her two young children.
  - Not:  on business.—to watch.
  - See Rule 53 for an abrupt break in thought.

- The new document—do you want to see it?—will
  exonerate my client.
  - See Rule 68 for a short question of three or fewer
    words within a sentence.
  - See Rule 69 for a long question within a sentence.

## Rule 62. Punctuation With a Closing Dash
Punctuation with a closing dash includes:

- <u>Period or Question Mark</u>. See Rule 61.

- <u>Comma</u>. When a closing dash occurs in a sentence where a comma would be required, use a closing dash and omit the comma.
    - The experiment was dangerous—much too risky—and management still approved it.
        - Not: too risky—, and management
        - A comma would be required per Rule 9.

- <u>Colon, Semicolon, or Closing Parenthesis</u>. When a closing dash occurs in a sentence where a colon, semicolon, or closing parenthesis would be required, use the punctuation mark and omit the closing dash.
    - I shipped a heavy box of books on different topics—all thick college textbooks: math, science, and history.
        - Not: college textbooks—: math, science
        - A colon is required per Rule 47.
    - The experiment was dangerous—much too risky; management still approved it.
        - Not: too risky—; management still
        - A semicolon is required per Rule 39.


# The Question Mark

## Rule 63. Direct Question
Use a question mark after a direct question.

- Did Zoey see the recent survey results?
- Do you recall seeing the car before the accident?
- What time did the meeting with the client end?
- Did Ava leave work after 5:00 p.m.?

Use one space after a question mark (Rule 126).

Capitalize the first word after a question mark (Rule 138).

Punctuate an indirect question with a period.

- Luis asked if Melinda will attend the meeting.

Punctuate each direct question with a question mark. See Rule 66 for a series of elliptical questions.

- Q  Was that conference on Monday or Tuesday? Did Tim attend the conference?
- Q  Who was driving? Was Tim driving?

Punctuate a direct question phrased like a statement with a question mark.

- Q  You left work at 5:00 p.m.?
  A  More like 5:15.

- Q  You recall seeing the truck before the accident?
  A  No.

## Rule 64. Statement Before or After a Direct Question
When an statement (independent clause) precedes or follows a direct question, punctuate them separately for clarity.

- Q  What time did you finish? I'm referring to the meeting on December 9, 2021.
- Q  Were you married? I mean at the time you moved to Montana.
- Q  Tom is a former co-worker. When did you first meet him?
- Q  You left work at 5:30 p.m. Do you recall?
  o  See Rule 67.

## Rule 65. Elliptical Question
Use a question mark after an elliptical question.

Like a fragment, an elliptical question is a grammatically incomplete question that represents a complete question.  Any missing sentence element is understood from the context

- When will you finish that assignment? **In a day or two?**
- Before the accident, were you walking? **Jogging?**
- What were you doing on the 12th of May? **Working?**

**Rule 66. Series of Connected Elliptical Questions**
Use a question mark after each elliptical question in a series of connected elliptical questions.

The words of each elliptical question can usually replace words in the original question. They are often suggested alternative answers.

- Were you walking? **Jogging? Running?**
- Was the car that hit you black? **Silver? White?**
- Did you attend an evening class that Monday? **That Wednesday? That Friday?**

Capitalization of connected elliptical questions is not required when the questions are brief and related to the original question's subject and verb. Because court reporting software is normally programmed to capitalize the first word after a question mark, many court reporters do not use lowercase with connected elliptical questions.

- Were you walking? Jogging? Running?
  - Or: Were you walking? jogging? running?
- Was the car that hit you black? Silver? White?
  - Or: Was the car that hit you black? silver? white?

**Rule 67. Short Question at the End of a Sentence**
Use a comma to separate a short direct question of three or fewer words at the end of a sentence that is grammatically incomplete. These types of questions are also known as *echo questions* or *tag questions*.

- Mr. Smith had leg surgery in 2015, right?
- Sarah needs the paperwork, correct?
- William is right, isn't he?
- You aren't required to buy the phone, are you?
- Angela dropped off the report, didn't she?

Use a period to separate a short and grammatically complete question at the end of a sentence (Rule 64).

- Sarah needs the paperwork. Is that correct?
- Angela dropped off the report. Do you recall?

**Rule 68. Short Question Within a Sentence**
Use commas to separate a short direct question of three or fewer words within a sentence. Place the question mark at the end of the sentence.

- Angela, can't she, drop off the report tomorrow?
  - Not: Angela, can't she?, drop off the report tomorrow.
- Mr. Smith had leg surgery, didn't he, in 2015?
  - Not: Mr. Smith had leg surgery, didn't he?, in 2025.
- Andrew saw the document, had he not, before today?


**Rule 69. Long Question Within a Sentence**
Use dashes to separate a long direct question of four or more words within a sentence. Place the question mark before the closing dash (Rule 61).

- The client's file—do you want a copy?—will answer all the questions.
- The couple tried—did they not try their best?—to find the lost dog.


**Rule 70. Long Question After an Opening Phrase**
Use a comma to separate a long question of four or more words that follows an opening phrase. Capitalize the first word of the question.

The opening phrase frequently ends with the word *is, are, was,* or *were.*

- The key question in the report was, Did the data confirm the hypotheses?
- The question is, Did you see the news report?
- Randell thought, What am I doing here?
- Local government leaders debated, How can we fund important services with limited funding?

**Rule 71. Long Question After an Independent Clause**
Use a colon to separate a long question of four or more words from an introductory independent clause. Capitalize the first word of the question.

- The report had one key question: Did the data confirm the hypotheses?
- The question is this: Did you see the news report?
- Local government leaders debated the topic: How can we fund important services with limited funding?

**Rule 72. Long Question Followed by a Phrase**
When a phrase follows a long question of four or more words, place a question mark after the long question and do not capitalize the phrase.

- Did the data confirm the hypotheses? was the key question in the report.
  - Not: the hypotheses? Was the
- Did you see the news report? is the question.
- What am I doing here? thought Randell.

# Quotation Marks

**Rule 73. Direct Quotation and Quotation Capitalization**
Enclose a direct quotation of a speaker or document in double quotation marks. Use double quotation marks whenever a speaker thinks their words are an exact record of a speaker or document.

Capitalize the first word of a direct quotation when it is the pronoun *I*, is a proper noun or adjective (see Rule 137), begins a complete sentence, or begins a line of poetry.

- Emma's parents said, "Yes."
- James replied, "Who said that lie?"
- She answered, "Bill, not Amy, illegally accessed the checking and savings account."
- The report states this: "Officers Branham and Ramirez arrived at 7:34 a.m. They search the backyard after the homeowner was contacted."

A direct quotation of a document should exactly match the original wording, spelling, capitalization, and punctuation—even if the original is incorrect. See Rule 124 about using "[*sic*]" with an important error that may confuse readers.

For omitted material in a quotation, use an ellipsis (Rule 118).

For added material to a quotation, use brackets (Rule 123).

<u>Beginning or Ending of Quotation Cannot Be Determined</u>:
Do <u>not</u> use double quotation marks when you cannot determine where a direct quotation begins or ends.

- Cassie said, He's a cheater. Trust me.
    - Is "Trust me" part of the direct quotation?

- Q   Officer Franklin asked if you saw the person who stole your car. You said, I think, yes.
    - Is "I think" part of the direct quotation?

<u>Single Quotation Marks</u>:
Use single quotation marks for a direct quotation of a speaker or document within a direct quotation of a speaker or document. When a double quotation mark directly follows a single quotation mark, add a space between them for clarity.

- Leon explained his nervousness, "Lisa said, 'Don't you dare run into me at the party.' "
    - Not:  at the party.'" (no quotation mark separation)

- The teacher said, "Let's dive into the context of the well-known phrase 'Letting someone off the hook.' "

**Rule 74. Signal Phrase With a Direct Quotation**
Separate an introductory, interrupting, or concluding "signal phrase" from a direct quotation with a comma or commas (see examples). Omit the comma if a period or question mark occurs where the comma would be placed.

Signal phrases include the verbs *said, asked, responded, stated, replied, yelled, screamed,* and similar verbs.

<u>Introductory Signal Phrase</u>:
Place a comma between the signal phrase and the opening quotation mark, but use a colon when the direct quotation is more than one sentence (Rule 75).

When a sentence continues after the quotation, separate it with a comma. Place the comma inside the closing quotation mark (Rule 78).

- The manager said, "It's time to go."
- Tammy's letter read, "I will fly to New York on Friday."
    - Or: letter read: "I will  (see Rule 75).
- Anya yelled, "Get out of here," and she dashed out of the conference room.
- The attorney asked, "Do you know her?" and pointed to the defendant.
    - Not:  know her?," and pointed  (comma omitted due to the question mark).

<u>Concluding Signal Phrase</u>:
Place a comma inside the closing quotation mark (Rule 78) and before the signal phrase.

- "It's time to go," the manager said.
- "Who said that lie?" James asked.
    - Not:  that lie?," James asked  (comma omitted due to the question mark).

<u>Interrupting Signal Phrase</u>:
Apply the above guidelines for an introductory and concluding signal phrase.

- "I'm traveling," Tom whispered, "to Chicago for business next week."
- "I really like the plan," Mary replied. "However, I have a few changes."
    - Comma after *replied* omitted due to the period.

<u>No Signal Phrase</u>:
- I disagree with Liam that we are just "evolved animals."
- The medical reference has "minimal side effects" with that dosage.

**Rule 75. Colon Before Direct Quotation**
Use a colon before a direct quotation when an independent clause introduces the direct quotation or when the direct quotation is more than one sentence.

Independent Clause Introduction:
- The judge gave the jury excellent instructions: "Gather the facts and decide the case in the deliberation room."
- I will always remember my father's advice: "Always do what you think is right."

Quotation Is More Than One Sentence:
- Ms. Anderson said: "I have heard enough, and you are beating around the bush. Please answer the question."
- The neighbor stated: "The police arrived around 7:30. They went into the backyard looking for a suspect."

Some court reporters prefer to use a colon to separate an introductory phrase from a direct quotation of a document. Using a colon instead of a comma is acceptable as long as the usage is consistent throughout the transcript.

- Tammy's letter read: "I will fly to New York on Friday."
- The report states: "Officers Branham and Ramirez arrived at 7:34 a.m."

**Rule 76. Punctuating the Words *Quote* and *Close Quote***
Separate any spoken punctuation (*quote, open quote, close quote, quote/unquote, period,* and so on) with commas. Include both the spoken punctuation and quotation marks in the transcript.

Include the spoken punctuation because a transcript is a verbatim record. Include quotation marks whenever a speaker thinks their words are an exact record of a speaker or document (see Rule 73).

- The manager said, quote: "Fire. Get out now."
- He said, quote/unquote, "I don't live there anymore."

- I told him to, quote, "solve," close quote, the problem.
  - Not: I told him to, quote, solve, close quote, the problem.
  - Not: I told him to "solve" the problem.

- The beginning of that section reads, quote, "The landlord shall mail the notice within thirty days."
  - Or: reads, quote: "The landlord  (see Rule 75).

- That restaurant has the best salads, period.


## Rule 77. Quotation Marks With Paragraphed Material

When a direct quotation is more than one paragraph, place an opening quotation mark at the start of each new paragraph and only one closing quotation mark at the end of the direct quotation in the last paragraph.

- The sign on the small drop box stated:
  "Your employment application should only contain:
  "1. Full name.
  "2. Work history of only company name and dates.
  "3. Contact phone number and email."

- Let me quote your previous testimony.
  "QUESTION: What time did you leave for work?
  "ANSWER: About 7:15 a.m.
  "QUESTION: How certain are you?
  "ANSWER: Within a few minutes."


## Rule 78. Closing Quotation Mark With a Period or Comma

Always place a period or comma inside a closing quotation mark.

- Lester shouted, "Hold the elevator."
- Mary used satire in her poem "Scorned."
- I recall saying, "It's a simple sentence."

- "Hold the elevator," Lester shouted.

- "It's a simple sentence," I recall saying.
- "Scorned," Mary said, "uses satire."

**Rule 79. Closing Quotation Mark With a Colon or Semicolon**
Place a colon or semicolon outside a closing quotation mark.

- They violated the "return policy"; I emailed the next day.
- The motto was "Efficiency"; now it is "Simplicity."
- In customer service calls, we include two things under "other": service visits and phone conversations.
- The survey concluded "the reason people use incorrect punctuation": too many rules.


**Rule 80. Closing Quotation Mark with a Dash
or Question Mark**
Place a dash or question mark inside a closing quotation mark when it is part of the original quotation. When it is not part of the original quotation, place it outside a closing quotation mark. When a question mark applies to both the original quotation and the sentence, place it inside the closing quotation mark.

Part of Original Quote:
- "Do you want your receipt?" the sales clerk asked.
- My attorney probed, "Did you sign that agreement?"
- The police report states, "I saw a hooded person—"
  - Or:  report states: "I saw  (see Rule 75)

Not Part of Original Quote:
- Who first yelled "fire"?
- Did Lester say, "Hold the elevator"?
- A  I heard the gang member say, "Let's murder"—
  Q  Those exact words?

Question Mark Applies to Quote and Sentence:
- Did the attorney ask, "Did you sign that agreement?"
- Did I already enquire, "Where do you currently work?"


**Rule 81. Word or Phrase Introduced by Words Like
*Called, Labeled, Marked,* or *Titled***
Enclose a word or phrase introduced by *called, entitled, known as, labeled, marked, named, signed,* or *titled* in double quotation marks.

- The document was marked "Top Secret."
- Tommy is known as "Lefty" in the neighborhood.
- The mysterious love letter was signed "Your Valentine."

## Rule 82. Title of a Book Chapter, Magazine Article, Song, or Poem

Use double quotation marks to enclose the title of a work within a larger work: book chapter, magazine article, newspaper article, song from an album, poem in a book, TV episode, web page, blog post, and so on. Also, use double quotation marks to enclose the title of an unpublished work.

- Have you read the magazine article "Heart Disease: Just the Facts"?
- My favorite *Twilight Zone* episode is "To Serve Man."
- Judy Garland sings "Somewhere Over the Rainbow" from *The Wizard of Oz.*

Italicize the title of a book, magazine, newspaper, movie, TV series, music album, website, or blog (Rule 131).

See Rule 139 for capitalization of a title or subtitle of a published, produced, or released work.


## Rule 83. Technical or Unusual Word Usage

Enclose a word or phrase in double quotation marks to emphasize it is used in a technical or unusual way. Use quotation marks with only the first occurrence.

Technical Usage:
- What does "final approval" include?
- In 1985 how did a person "boot" a computer?

Unusual Usage:
The word or phrase is often used in an ironic or humorous way.

- Some call it a tax. I call it "revenue augmentation."
- On the exam, the "class genius" got a D.
- Q   Did you hire Nick to kill your boss?
  A   I only asked him to "solve" a problem.

Do <u>not</u> use double quotation marks with a word or phrase introduced by *so-called*.

- On the exam, the so-called class genius got a D.
  o   Not:  the so-called "class genius" got
- The so-called training was a sales pitch.

**Rule 84. Slang, Mispronunciations, and Made-Up Words**
Handle slang, mispronounced words, or made-up words in the following manner.

<u>Slang</u>:
Do <u>not</u> enclose slang or a colloquial expression in double quotation marks.

- What **merch** does the website sell?
  - o  Not:  What "merch" does
- Q  What did he wear what evening?
  A  He wore a tailored suit and some **sick** shoes.
    - o  Not:  some "sick" shoes

<u>Mispronounced Words</u>:
When a word is mispronounced and the mispronunciation is unimportant, write the correct word. When the mispronunciation is important, write the word phonetically (see Rule 125).

- I was hit with **nunchucks**.
  - o  Speaker said numchucks.
  - o  Unimportant mispronunciation.
- Do you like Billie **Eilish's** "Happier Than Ever"?
  - o  Speaker said Ay-lish, not Eye-lish.
  - o  Unimportant mispronunciation.
- Ben loves burritos from **Chipotle**.
  - o  Speaker said Chih-pol-tay, not Chih-poht-lay.
  - o  Unimportant mispronunciation
- Q  Are you currently taking any medications?
  A  I'm taking **Ga-gaw-tin** [phonetic].
    - o  Important mispronunciation. Write phonetically.
  Q  Gabapentin?
  A  Yes, Gabapentin.

<u>Made-Up Words</u>:
Enclose a made-up word in double quotation marks. Use quotation marks with only the first occurrence.

- Those are "absitively" my feelings.
- Ryan's "fauxpology" came after several excuses.
- After the marketing plan failed, the "blamestorming" emails began.

## Rule 85. Nickname or Pseudonym

When a nickname or pseudonym appears alone or in place of the first name, capitalize it (see Rule 137). If the nickname or pseudonym appears between the first name and last name, enclose it in double quotation marks.

- Did Eldrick "Tiger" Woods win the Masters in 2005?
- Tiger Woods has won the Masters five times.
- Calamity Jane was a well-known sharpshooter.
- Martha "Calamity" Jane Cannary was born in 1852.
- When did Babe Ruth hit his first home run?
- George "Babe" Ruth Jr. hit his first professional home run in 1914.

## Rule 86. Definition of a Word or Phrase

Enclose the dictionary definition of a word or phrase in double quotation marks. Italicize the word or phrase being defined (Rule 134).

- Per the dictionary, a *schedule* can mean "a written or printed list, catalog, or inventory."

- Q   What did you mean by "approval"?
  A   I used the dictionary definition for *approval* of "to give official authorization."

## Rule 87. Translation of a Word or Phrase

Enclose a translation of a word or phrase in double quotation marks. Italicize the word or phrase being translated.

- The Latin phrase *Vox populi* translates in English to "voice of the people."

- *La citudad y los perros*, literally translated is "the city and the dogs," was published in 1963 with the title *The Time of the Hero*.
  - Acceptable: *los perros*—literally translated is "the city and the dogs"—was published  (Rule 53).

See Rule 133 about using italics with an unfamiliar foreign word or phrase.

# The Apostrophe

**Rule 88. Possessive Form of a Singular Word**
Write the possessive form of a singular word by adding an apostrophe and *s*. Do not change the spelling of the word.

- The defendant's testimony is pure perjury.
- Andrew borrowed his friend's car to get to work.
- Unfortunately, I did not follow my lawyer's instructions.
- There is something wrong with the apple's taste.

For a word ending in a *s* or *z* sound, write what is spoken. When the speaker adds an additional *s* or *z* sound to the word (the likely case), add an apostrophe and *s*. When only the original *s* or *z* sound is spoken, add only an apostrophe.

- The witness's testimony was pure perjury.
  - Two *s* sounds spoken (original plus additional).
- The business's profit dropped sharply last month.
  - Two *s* sounds spoken (original plus additional).
- Mr. Jones' wallet was stolen last night.
  - Only one *z* sound spoken (the original).
- Mr. Jones's wallet was stolen last night.
  - Two *z* sounds spoken (original plus additional).

**Rule 89. Possessive Form of a Plural Word**
Write the possessive form of a plural word ending in *s* (the typical case) by adding an apostrophe. Write the possessive form of a plural word not ending in *s* by adding an apostrophe and *s*. Do not change the spelling of the word in either case.

Plural Word Ending in "s":
- The profit did not meet investors' expectations.
- A recent email summarized ten companies' AI policy.
- The lockout violated workers' rights.
- As I ran past, pairs of dogs' eyes tracked me.

Plural Word Not Ending in "s":
- Is women's intuition a myth or reality?
- The next school board meeting will discuss the new law on children's educational requirements.

## Rule 90. Possessive Form of a Compound Noun

Write the possessive form of a compound noun using Rule 88 (singular word) or Rule 89 (plural word). Do not change the spelling of the word. Write what is spoken.

- Per the salesperson's opinion, the dress is overpriced.
- I borrowed my sister-in-law's car to get to work.
- The crime scene raised the passerby's anxiety level.
- Law enforcement froze the double-dipper's bank account during the financial investigation.

The plural of a compound noun is normally formed by making the main part of the compound noun plural (salespersons, sisters-in-law, passersby, double-dippers).


## Rule 91. Possessive Form of a Business or Personal Name

Write the possessive form of a business or personal name using Rule 88 (singular word) or Rule 89 (plural word). Do not change the spelling of the name. Write what is spoken.

- A celebrity attended NewLeaf's grand opening.
- Art Happiness's downtown location is closed.
  - Two *s* sounds spoken (original plus additional).
- Kim's father retired in March.
- Kim Smith's father retired in March.
- The Smiths' father retired in March.
- The Rodriguez' oldest son moved to New York.
  - Only one *z* sound spoken (the original).
- The Rodriguezes' oldest son moved to New York.
  - Two *z* sounds spoken (original plus additional).
- The Reynolds' car was broken into last night.
  - Only one *z* sound spoken (the original).
- The Reynolds's car was broken into last night.
  - Two *z* sounds spoken (original plus additional).

When a business or personal name ends in a number or abbreviation (see Rule 25 and Rule 34), write the possessive form by adding an apostrophe and *s*.

- Jeffcott & Co.'s stock dropped sharply yesterday.
- Farm Supply Inc.'s supply of corn feed is stable.
- John Hyde Jr.'s father lives in Kansas.
- Ron William III's birthday party is this Thursday.


## Rule 92. Joint vs. Separate Possession

Because a person may misspeak or not know how to show joint versus separate possession, write what is spoken using Rule 88 (singular word) or Rule 89 (plural word).

When two subjects share one verb (compound subject), they can have either joint or separate possession. Joint possession means both subjects mutually have the object. Separate possession means each subject has its own object.

To show joint possession, a person should use the possessive form with only the final item or person.

- Rebecca and Mason's large painting is in the art exhibit.
  - Rebecca and Mason jointly possess (and maybe produced) the object (the large painting).
- Todd joined the fraternity against his mother and father's repeated advice.
  - The mother and father had the same advice.

To show separate possession, a person should use the possessive form with each item or person.

- Rebecca's and Mason's painting technique is similar.
  - Rebecca and Mason have separate objects (painting technique) that are similar.
- Todd joined the fraternity against his mother's and his father's repeated advice.
  - The mother and father had separate advice, though both were against Todd joining the fraternity. The repeated *his* signals and reinforces the separate objects (the advice).

## Rule 93. Incomplete Possessive

The noun a possessive word describes may be missing (not spoken) because it is understood from the context. Write the possessive form using Rule 88 (singular word) or Rule 89 (plural word).

- Shantell has a bachelor's in accounting.
  - *Degree* omitted (bachelor's degree).
- The doctor's called to schedule an appointment.
  - *Office* omitted (doctor's office).
- This week's game was better than last week's.
  - *Game* omitted (last week's game).

## Rule 94. Possessive in an "of" Phrase

Use Rule 88 (singular word) or Rule 89 (plural word) to write the possessive form of a word in an "of" phrase.

Normally, the object in an "of" phrase (a prepositional phrase) should not be in the possessive form. This idiomatic use of the possessive form is called a *double possessive.*

- The cellphone of the plaintiff's was seized as evidence.
- A lifelong quest of Lilly's is to find a four-leaf clover.
- Robert is a childhood friend of my aunt's.

## Rule 95. Consecutive Possessive Words

When two or more consecutive words are each spoken in the possessive form, use Rule 88 (singular word) or Rule 89 (plural word) to write each possessive form. Write what is spoken.

A string of spoken words in possessive form can sound awkward. It has been referred to as a *possessive pileup.*

- I could not believe my eyes. The neighbor's house's door was painted bright orange.
- Lynette will be visiting her husband's sister's daughter in early April.
- Did you read the department's director's email about timesheet approval?

## Rule 96. Some Expressions Involving Time, a Monetary Amount, or Distance

Some expressions involving time, distance, or a monetary amount use the possessive form. Use Rule 88 (singular word) or Rule 89 (plural word) to write the possessive form.

While these expressions use the possessive form, they do not show possession. Often the possessive form can be thought of as meaning "of" (*a day's work* means *a day of work*).

- The severance pay is only one week's salary.
- The fire wiped out three years' progress toward the restoration of the historic building.
- In this economy, you need to get every dollar's worth.
- The thief stole several hundred dollars' worth of copper.
- The project will progress smoothly if Tim is kept at arm's length.
- The famous Santa Cruz Mystery Spot is only a three miles' drive from here.

## Rule 97. Personal and Indefinite Possessive Pronouns

Do <u>not</u> use an apostrophe with the possessive form of a personal pronoun: *my, mine, our, ours, you, yours, his, her, hers, its, their,* and *theirs.* For indefinite pronouns that have a possessive form, use Rule 88 (singular word) or Rule 89 (plural word) to write the possessive form.

The following frequently used indefinite pronouns have a possessive form. Write what is spoken.

| | | |
|---|---|---|
| another | either | one |
| anybody | everyone | other |
| anybody else | everyone else | somebody |
| anyone | neither | somebody else |
| anyone else | no one | someone |
| each one | no one else | someone else |
| everybody | nobody | |
| everybody else | nobody else | |

The following frequently used indefinite pronouns do <u>not</u> have a possessive form. Write what is spoken.

| | | |
|---|---|---|
| all | many | several |
| any | most | some |
| both | much | something |
| each | none | such |
| few | nothing | this |

## Rule 98. Possessive or Descriptive Word?

To determine if a word is a possessive or descriptive word, rewrite as an *of* phrase and as a *for* phrase. If the *of* phrase better matches the meaning, use an apostrophe. If the *for* phrase better matches the meaning, do not use an apostrophe.

- The **Reynolds** car   OR   the **Reynolds'** car?
  - o   Rewrite with *of*:   car of the Reynolds   (most likely)
  - o   Rewrite with *for*:   car for the Reynolds   (possible)
  - o   Conclusion:        Reynolds' (possessive)

- The new **leaders** guide   OR   the new **leaders'** guide?
  - o   Rewrite with *of*:   guide of new leaders   (possible)
  - o   Rewrite with *for*:   guide for new leaders  (most likely)
  - o   Conclusion:        leaders (descriptive)

- The **girls** softball team   OR   the **girls'** softball team?
  - o   Rewrite with *of*:   softball team of girls   (most likely)
  - o   Rewrite with *for*:   softball team for girls  (possible)
  - o   Conclusion:        girls' (possessive)

Another method to help determine if a word is a possessive or a descriptive word is to insert an adjective (*old, new, large, small, first, last, red, blue,* and so on) between the possessive/descriptive word and the noun. If an adjective can be sensibly inserted, use an apostrophe. If not, do not use an apostrophe.

- The **Reynolds** car   OR   the **Reynolds'** car?
  - o   Insert adjective:  The Reynolds' *new* car.  (Yes)
  - o   Conclusion:        Reynolds' (possessive)

- The new **leaders** guide  OR  the new **leaders'** guide?
  - ○ Insert adjective:  The new leaders *blue* guide  (No)
    - ▪ Should be:  The *blue* new leaders guide
  - ○ Conclusion:  leaders (descriptive)


## Rule 99. Plural of a Lowercase or Uppercase Letter

Add an apostrophe and *s* to form a plural of a lowercase or uppercase letter. Adding only *s* to form the plural of an uppercase letter is acceptable, but it is not recommended where readability is sufficiently reduced.

Lowercase Letter:
Italicize a lowercase letter used as a letter (Rule 135).

- Please mind your *p*'s and *q*'s.
- You spelled *committee* with one too many *m*'s.
- Wilber had two small *x*'s in red ink across his face.

Uppercase Letter:

- The word is misspelled. It contains two T's.
  - ○ Acceptable:  contains two Ts

- Wilber had two large X's in red ink across his face.
  - ○ Acceptable:  two large Xs in red

- In real estate, the three L's are location, location, and location.
  - ○ Acceptable (not recommended):  three Ls are


## Rule 100. Plural of a Likely Misread Word

Add an apostrophe and *s* to form the plural of any word likely to be misread.

- The or's in the sentence should be ands.
- I researched all tenant move-in's for last year
- The which's and that's in the sentence are misused.


Nouns made from other parts of speech generally form the plural by adding *s* or *es*. Per the *Merriam-Webster.com Dictionary*:

| | |
|---|---|
| ands, ifs, and buts | ups and downs |
| dos and don'ts | pros and cons |
| ins and outs | yeses and nos |

## Rule 101. Omission of Letters or Figures

Use an apostrophe to show one or more omitted letters or figures. Use a closing mark ('), not an opening mark ('), at the location of the omitted letters or figures.

- My son was born in April '97.
  - Spoken: April ninety-seven.
  - See Rule 171 for date formatting.
- I bought the condo in 2011 or '12.
  - Spoken: two thousand eleven or twelve.
- I love rock 'n' roll.
  - Not: rock 'n' roll. (The first apostrophe should be a closing mark, not an opening mark.)
- Have you tried Shake 'n Bake chicken?
  - Follow the official product spelling and style by consulting a Merriam-Webster dictionary or the company website. In this case, the apostrophe style appears to be an opening mark.

## Rule 102. Formation of Certain Verbs

Add an apostrophe before a verbal suffix (*'s, 'ing, 'd*) to form the verb of a letter, number, or abbreviation.

- The investigation showed the person OD'ing Friday night, not Saturday morning.
- The detective star 69'd the landline phone to reach the last-called person.
- Jan is sick, so she x'd her European vacation.

Write the full form of the verb when available. For example, use *okays, okaying,* or *okayed*—not *ok's, ok'ing,* or *ok'd*.

While a Merriam-Webster dictionary may list a verb form with a hyphen or without an apostrophe, it always includes the apostrophe form. The *Merriam-Webster.com Dictionary* lists the following:

| | |
|---|---|
| cc'd | cc'ing |
| ID'd, Ided | ID'ing, Iding |
| OD'd, Oded | OD'ing (and OD's) |
| OK'd, ok'd | OK'ing, ok'ing |
| x'd, x-ed, xed | x'ing, x-ing |

## Rule 103. Contractions
Use an apostrophe in contractions.

Common contractions include the following:

| | | | | |
|---|---|---|---|---|
| aren't | don't | I've | that's | who's |
| can't | he's | it's | they'll | won't |
| couldn't | I'd | let's | they're | you'll |
| didn't | I'll | she's | wasn't | you're |
| doesn't | I'm | shouldn't | what's | you've |


# The Hyphen

## Rule 104. Common Prefixes and Suffixes
Add most prefixes and suffixes to a word without a hyphen to form a closed word.

Prefix:
- The accident occurred **midblock**.
- What did the **postmortem** reveal?
- **Multitasking** is important for any career.

Suffix:
- The wind moved the tall grass in **wavelike** motions.
- What are the new **statewide** laws?
- Cleaning the bathroom is a **thankless** job.

Use a hyphen with the following prefixes and suffixes:
- **co-** (before an *o* starting word) co-owner, co-opt
  But: coordinate, cooperate
- **ex-** (meaning *former*) ex-convict, ex-husband
- **great-** (family title) great-aunt, great-grandfather
- **quasi-** quasi-judicial, quasi-legal, quasi-governmental
- **self-** self-evident, self-serving, self-worth
- **-in-law** (family title) brother-in-law, mother-in-law
- **-odd** (often with *some*) 30-odd plastic pieces, 50 some-odd people (see Rule 191)
- **-old** centuries-old, 5-year-old (see Rule 179)
- **-plus** 40-plus people, million-plus budget

The following suffixes do <u>not</u> use a hyphen. However, a hyphen <u>may</u> be needed for a situation requiring increased readability (see Rule 106). Using a hyphen is more likely when the word and suffix end in the same letter or when the suffix creates three back-to-back vowels or consonants.

- **-ish**    lazyish, eightish, smallish, stylish, yellowish
- **-like**    catlike, childlike, jellylike, humanlike
  - Use a hyphen when *like* is part of an adjective: prison-like workplace (Rule 110).
- **-type**    archetype, haplotype, prototype, subtype
  - Use a hyphen when *type* is part of an adjective: commuter-type car (Rule 110).
- **-wide**    citywide, nationwide, statewide, storewide
- **-wise**    clockwise, edgewise, lengthwise, streetwise
  - Use a hyphen when *wise* is part of an adjective: recovery-wise plan  (Rule 110).

- I would describe the construction as tent-type.
- Thumbscrew-wise tighten the gear assembly.
- Q   How old is your dog, Kona?
  A   Seven. We got him around three-ish.


**Rule 105. Prefix or Suffix to a Number or Capitalized Word**
Use a hyphen to join a prefix or suffix to a number or capitalized word.

Number:
- Where is the pre-1900s machine exhibit?
- Sonya made a 1976-like outfit for Halloween.
- The graph shows the post-2008 economic recovery.
- Did the 1950-style diner open yet?

Capitalized Word:
- Who won the mid-June elections?
- That statement is anti-American.
- My roommate loves Chicago-style pizza.
- The December-like weather came early this year.

**Rule 106. Prefix or Suffix to a Word That Could Be Misread**
Use a hyphen to join a prefix or suffix to a word that could be misread. Common situations include the following:

- The **ultra-apathetic** student unplugged the alarm clock.
  - A double "a" combination requires a hyphen.

- My doctor suggested an **anti-inflammatory** medication.
  - A double "i" combination requires a hyphen.

- The water is **un-ionized**.
  - A hyphen is required because *unionized* has a different meaning.
  - Use a hyphen when the added prefix or suffix creates a conflict (same spelling, different meaning).

- Do we need to **re-create** the scene?
  - A hyphen is required because *recreate* has a different meaning.
  - Other *re-* starting words that could be misread:

| | |
|---|---|
| re-act, react | re-press, repress |
| re-charge, recharge | re-search, research |
| re-collect, recollect | re-sent, resent |
| re-cover, recover | re-serve, reserve |
| re-dress, redress | re-side, reside |
| re-form, reform | re-sign, resign |
| re-lease, release | re-solve, resolve |
| re-mark, remark | re-treat, retreat |

- The requirement is in the **sub-subparagraph**.
  - A doubled prefix requires a hyphen.

- The ad stated it was "**post-self-cleaning**."
  - A prefix to a hyphenated word requires a hyphen.

- The list had successful **non-high school** graduates.
  - A prefix to an open compound requires a hyphen.
  - Both the prefix and open compound may be hyphenated (non-high-school graduates) when it is a compound adjective and the situation needs increased readability (see Rule 109).

- The new employee was eager but **skill-less**.
  - A suffix with tripled consonants requires a hyphen. Common situations include *-less* and *-like*.

**Rule 107. Suspending Hyphens**
Use a suspending hyphen with each prefix, suffix, word, or number that applies to the following (or preceding) hyphenated word.

- I bought certified deposits for 12- and 24-month terms.
- Alexia has 9-, 11-, and 14-year-old children.
- My pre- and post-op anxiety levels were off the chart.
- I would guess George is twenty-one or -two.


**Rule 108. Compound Noun, Verb, or Adjective**
Check a Merriam-Webster dictionary to determine if a compound noun, verb, or adjective is written in an open, closed, or hyphenated format (see Rule 130). When a word is not listed in the dictionary, consult similar entries.

A compound word consists of two or more words that work together to express a single idea. The compound word can function as a noun, verb, or adjective.

<u>Compound Noun</u>:
Many compound nouns listed in the dictionary are written in either a closed or hyphenated format.

When a compound noun is not listed in the dictionary and similar entries are a mix of closed and hyphenated formats, a closed format is preferred unless the closed format would be harder to read. When there are no similar entries or you are unsure how to write the compound noun, traditional guidance is to write as separate words (open format).

- Angela did a **run-through** of the new system.
- The malfunctioning ATM caused a **free-for-all**.
  - Hyphenate when no nouns are in the compound.
- My **brother-in-law** is a **know-it-all**.
- Katie retired after 30 years as an **copywriter-editor**.
  - Hyphenate when the nouns show one person or thing has two functions.
  - A slash may be appropriate (see Rule 119).
- Does Sonia currently work as a **stockbroker**?
- I selected **African American** on the application form.
  - Write a compound nationality as an open compound.

<u>Compound Verb</u>:
Many compound verbs listed in the dictionary are written in either a closed or hyphenated format.

- The thief **strong-armed** my purse from me.
- Did you **test-drive** the car before buying it?
- I **downloaded** the latest software update.
- She **proofread** the final draft of the book.

<u>Compound Adjective</u>:
See Rule 109 and Rule 110 for compound adjective guidance.

- I work in the **high-rise** building on Main Street.
- She invented a **time-saving** gadget.
- Did you attend many **high school** dances?
- My retirement funds are in a **money market** account.

## Rule 109. Identifying a Compound Adjective

If the words before a noun work together to express a single idea, they form a compound adjective. Consult a Merriam-Webster dictionary to determine if the compound adjective is written in an open, closed, or hyphenated format (see Rule 108).

See Rule 23 about coordinate or cumulative adjectives.

See Rule 110 for a compound adjective not in the dictionary.

<u>Compound Adjective Test</u>:
To determine if the words "work together" before a noun, check them separately and jointly. Does each word by itself sensibly describe the noun? Or do the words together form a single idea that sensibly describes the noun? Use these two useful tests to identify a compound adjective.

- Brad Pitt is a **well known** actor.
  - <u>Do the words describe separately</u>? No for "well actor." Yes for "known actor."
  - <u>Do the words describe together</u>? Yes, "well known" expresses a single idea describing the noun.
  - <u>Conclusion</u>: compound adjective.
  - <u>Dictionary</u>: hyphenated (well-known)

- I live on the eighth floor in a **ten story** building.
  - <u>Do the words describe separately</u>? No for "ten building." No for "story building."
  - <u>Do the words describe together</u>? Yes, "ten story" expresses a single idea describing the noun.
  - <u>Conclusion</u>: compound adjective
  - <u>Dictionary</u>: hyphenated (ten-story)

- The report covers the effects of **second hand** smoke.
  - <u>Do the words describe separately</u>? No for "second smoke." No for "hand smoke."
  - <u>Do the words describe together</u>? Yes, "second hand" expresses a single idea describing the noun.
  - <u>Conclusion</u>: compound adjective
  - <u>Dictionary</u>: closed (secondhand)

**Rule 110. Compound Adjective Not Listed in the Dictionary**
When a compound adjective is not listed in the dictionary, hyphenate it unless it includes (1) an adverb ending in *-ly*; (2) a proper noun; (3) the adverb *more, most, less, least,* or *very*; (4) a chemical term; (5) a percentage; (6) a foreign phrase; or (7) a number or letter as a second element.

Adverb Ending in *-ly:*
- Sophia is a **highly valued** employee.
- Is this a **poorly written** sentence?
- Logan joined the **newly formed** business.

Proper Noun:
- The deal took a **New York** minute.
- The **Supreme Court** decision will be issued tomorrow.
- Peter studies **Middle Eastern** languages at Yale.

Adverbs *More, Most, Less, Least,* or *Very:*
- I cannot decide who is the **more determined** person.
- Is punctuation the **least interesting** topic?
- Hailey's **very thoughtful** comment emphasized the immediate needs and how everyone could help.

Chemical Term:
- A **sodium chloride** solution ruined my jeans.
- The **amino acid** reaction created a salt.

A Percentage:
- The March 2020 stay-at-home order caused a **50 percent** reduction in vehicle traffic.
- Clinical trials showed the medication caused a **10 percent** increase in blood pressure.

Foreign Phrase:
If the original foreign phrase contains hyphens, keep them. See Rule 133 for using italics with an unfamiliar foreign phrase.

- An *a priori* argument is deductive.
- The couple saved for the **in vitro** fertilization cost.
- Mom and Dad used a ***tête-à-tête*** approach for family finances.
  - The original foreign phrase has hyphens.

A Number or Letter as a Second Element:
See Rule 183 for a numbered reference.

- Liam wears a **size 10** shoe.
- Nearly 10 percent of Americans have **Type 2** diabetes.
- Did all **Group B** participants sign the waiver?


**Rule 111. Long Compound Adjective**
A compound adjective that is long (four or more words) or that could be misread <u>may</u> be enclosed in quotation marks. Both the hyphenated and quotation mark format are correct.

As a compound adjective increases in length, the more likely using quotation marks is a better choice for readability.

- Vivian's "I'm going out of my freaking mind" expression scared me.
  - Acceptable:  I'm-going-out-of-my-freaking-mind
- His head did a slow "you can't make me do it" shake.
  - Acceptable:  you-can't-make-me-do-it.
- Our conversation began with "how was your day?" stuff.
  - Acceptable:  how-was-your-day?

## Rule 112. Spelled-Out Words

Use a hyphen between the letters of a spelled-out word.

Use a space between words, and capitalize words or letters that are normally capitalized (see Rule 137 and Rule 192). If spelling is interrupted, separate it with a comma or commas. When part of a word is spelled out, use a hyphen only between the letters that are spelled out.

- My name is Cyndi Smith, C-y-n-d-i Smith.
- My last name is McDougall, M-c-D-o-u-g-a-l-l.
- My last name is McDougall, M-c, capital D-o-u-g-a-l-l.
- My last name is McDougall, M-c-D, as in dog, o-u-g-a-l-l.
- My last name is McDougall, M-c-D-o-u-g-a, double l.
- My best friend is Katty, t-t-y.

## Rule 113. The Words *Full-Time*, *Part-Time*, *Uh-Huh*, *Uh-Uh*, and *X-Ray*

The correct spelling of the following words are presently *full-time, part-time, uh-huh, uh-uh,* and *X-ray*.

Use the most recent edition of a Merriam-Webster dictionary for word spelling (Rule 130). Presently, the *Merriam-Webster.com Dictionary* lists *X-ray* (noun and adjective), *x-ray* (verb, preferred), and X-ray (verb, acceptable). Using *X-ray* for all cases is recommended.

- Do you work full-time or part-time?
- The doctor confirmed my broken toe with an X-ray.
- Please speak up and say yes or no. Do not say uh-huh or uh-uh.

## Rule 114. Exhibit Subpart

In an exhibit label, use a hyphen between an exhibit number and any subpart letter. Capitalize the word *Exhibit*.

Using sequential numbers to label exhibits is preferred. However, use the preference of the attorney or court for labeling, such as using numbers for the plaintiff and letters for the defendant.

When an exhibit has subparts, use a hyphen plus a sequential letter after the exhibit number to indicate the subpart (1-A, 1-B, 1-C, 1-D, and so on).

- Please mark this additional diagram as "Exhibit 1-B."
  - See Rule 81 about using double quotation marks.
- Is Exhibit 12-E the email sent on December 12?
- The exhibits in question are Exhibit 5-A, 5-B, and 5-C.
  - Spoken: 5A, 5B, and 5C.
- The exhibits in question are Exhibit 5-A, -B, and -C.
  - Spoken: 5A, B, and C.
- The exhibits in question are Exhibit 5-A through -C.
  - Spoken: 5A through C.


## Rule 115. Letter Used as a Prefix or Adjective

Use a hyphen when a letter is used as a prefix or adjective.

Use the most recent edition of a Merriam-Webster dictionary for word spelling (Rule 130).

- Rolando U-turned the car after passing his destination.
- I made an illegal U-ey to follow the suspect.
- The defendant T-boned my client at a T-intersection.
- That Ford Mustang has a V-8 engine.
- Is my V-neck sweater on my L-shaped desk?
- The T-cells are key for immune response.


## Rule 116. Military Pay Grade

Use a hyphen with a military pay grade (E-2, W-1, O-3, and so forth). Capitalize the pay grade letter.

A military pay grade is not a military rank, like Private, Sergeant, or Captain. Pay grades are administrative classifications used to standardize compensation across the six military branches. "E" stands for *Enlisted*, "O" for *Commissioned Officers*, and "W" for *Warrant Officers*.

- Are you currently an E-4 or -5?
  - Spoken: E 4 or 5.
- I was just promoted to an O-3 in June.
- What is the pay difference between E-5 and W-2?

See Rule 140 for capitalization of a military title before a name.

# The Ellipsis

## Rule 117. Speaker Trail-Off

Use an ellipsis (three spaced periods) to show when a speaker trails off and does not complete the thought or sentence.

- Q  You and Brenda took the car?
  A  We were just trying to . . .

- Q  What happened after the meeting?
  A  I left for lunch, paid for parking, and . . .

Use a dash to show speaker interruption (see Rule 54).


## Rule 118. Omitted Material Within a Direct Quotation

Use an ellipsis to show omitted material within a direct quotation of a speaker or document. Write an ellipsis as three spaced periods with a space before and after the periods.

- "The accident was caused by . . . the defendant."
- "The contract term . . . shall be . . . four years from the date of approval."

Add a period before an ellipsis to show the words before and after the ellipsis form a complete sentence, even if parts of the sentences are omitted.

- "The accident was caused by driver error. . . . In this case, the evidence points to the defendant."
  o  Complete sentences before and after the ellipsis.

- "The contract term is four years. . . . Extensions shall not exceed one year."
  o  Complete sentences before and after the ellipsis.

Do not use an ellipsis before the first word of the direct quotation unless the quotation begins midsentence. Do not use an ellipsis after the last word of the direct quotation unless the quotation is intentionally left incomplete.

- The report states, ". . . by driver error is the sole cause."
  o  The quotation begins midsentence.
  o  Or: states: ". . . by driver  (see Rule 75)

- The paragraph begins, "The contract term is . . ."
  o  The quotation is intentionally incomplete.
  o  Or: begins: "The contract  (see Rule 75)

# The Slash

### Rule 119. Separate Alternatives
Use a slash to separate alternatives.

Do not use a space before or after the slash unless an alternative is an open compound (see third example).

- The classic car had the original AM/FM tuner.
- The menu offered the choice of soup and/or salad.
- My father loved the Korean War / Vietnam War exhibit.
- Tammy screamed into the phone, quote/unquote, "I don't live there anymore."
- Both countries dispute the east/west border.
  - If the paired terms function as an adjective, a hyphen may be a better choice (east-west border). See Rule 109 and Rule 110.

See Rule 171 for using slash with a date.

See Rule 181 for using a slash with a fraction.

See Rule 186 for using a slash between consecutive years.

# Parentheses

### Rule 120. Explanatory Information
Enclose explanatory information in parentheses. Capitalize the first word, and place the period inside the closing parenthesis.

- (There was a discussion off the record.)
- (Exhibit 3 was marked for identification.)
- (Recess from 12:30 p.m. until 1:37 p.m.)
- (Proceedings concluded at 4:19 p.m.)
- (Jury in at 9:48 a.m.)
- (The reporter read the previous question.)
- (See Exhibit 5, line 4.)

## Rule 121. Witness Gestures

Enclose a witness gesture in parentheses. The description of the gesture should be impartial. Capitalize the first word, and place the period inside the closing parenthesis.

A gesture is a non-verbal response to a question. When a witness gives both a verbal answer and a gesture, write the verbal answer. The attorney is responsible for asking the witness to verbalize a gesture.

- Q   Where in the intersection did the accident occur?
  A   (Witness indicated on Exhibit 11.)

- Q   Please mark where you fell.
  A   (Witness marked Exhibit 8.)

- Q   Why did you go to the ER on March 17?
  A   (Witness pointed to their right knee.)

- Q   When preparing for the trip, did you gas up the car?
  A   Yes.
  Q   Did you check the engine fluids?
  A   (Witness shook their head.)
  Q   Is that yes or no?
  A   Yes.


## Rule 122. Sentence Element With Internal Commas

A dash normally separates a sentence element with internal commas that requires separation with punctuation (Rule 58). However, use parentheses when dashes would be confusing (usually dashes are used elsewhere in the sentence) or when parentheses noticeably improve readability.

- We (Tom from Lee's Law Group; Sue from Carter, Watson & White; and Bill from Murphy and Sons LLP) formed the super—correction—combined legal team for the prominent client who lives in Spokane, Washington.

- In major three cities (Chicago, Illinois; Detroit, Michigan; and New York City, New York), crime decreased last quarter—mostly for the better.

# Brackets

**Rule 123. Change or Comment Within a Direct Quotation**
Use brackets to enclose a change or comment within a direct quotation of a speaker or document.

A quotation of a document should exactly match the original wording, spelling, capitalization, and punctuation (Rule 73).

- Section 703, expressly declares that "[e]xcept as otherwise provided by statute, a public employee is liable for injurious acts or omissions."
  - The word *except* is capitalized in Section 703.
- The website states, ". . . [F]atigue is a common MS symptom."
  - The word *fatigue* is not capitalized on the website.
  - Or: website states: ". . . [F]atigue is  (Rule 75).
  - See Rule 118 for ellipsis usage.

A comment consisting of a word or short phrase should only be inserted into a direct quotation when it is absolutely necessary to clarify the meaning. The context nearly always provides enough information for the meaning.

- Margie said, "[Ray] Clark's smile always breaks the ice."
- "I married that year [2017]," Cody replied.
- The deposition stated, "The [new trial] order was issued three days later."
  - Or: deposition stated: "The [new trial]  (Rule 75)

**Rule 124. Using "[*sic*]" to Show an Error**
Only use "[*sic*]" with an important error in a direct quotation of a document that may confuse the reader.

A direct quotation of a document should exactly match the original wording, spelling, capitalization, and punctuation—even if the original is incorrect (Rule 73).

Using "[*sic*]" (Latin for "in this manner") shows the error is in the original document text and not your transcript. The word "[*sic*]" is italicized, if possible, and enclosed in brackets.

The court reporter needs the original document text to know if an error occurred. Without the original text, the court reporter writes what is spoken without using "[*sic*]." Further, an attorney is responsible to correct or point out any error in the document: misidentification, wrong word or number, and so on.

Guidelines for using "[*sic*]":
- Only use "[*sic*]" with a direct quotation of a document, not with a direct quotation of a speaker.
- Do not use "[*sic*]" with every error.
  - Only use "[*sic*]" with an important error that may confuse the reader. Its usage should be minimal.
- Do not use "[*sic*]" when the error is corrected or pointed out by a witness or attorney.
- For a recurring error requiring "[*sic*]," only use "[*sic*]" with the first occurrence.
- Instead of using "[*sic*]," consider inserting a clarifying word or short phrase in brackets (see Rule 123).
- For multiple (different) errors requiring "[*sic*]," use "[verbatim text]" or a similar note before the quotation instead of adding "[*sic*]" throughout the quotation.
  - Example: The email states [verbatim text]: "On . . .

Examples:
- <u>Situation</u>: At a videotaped deposition, the videographer reads the wrong address at the read-on. Should you use "[*sic*]"?
  - No. It is not a direct quotation of a document. Also, an attorney should have corrected the error.
- <u>Situation</u>: A witness said Exhibit 5, and the person meant Exhibit 4. Should you use "[*sic*]"?
  - No. It is not a direct quotation of a document. Also, an attorney should have corrected the error.
- <u>Situation</u>: A witness said "Magnum Street" throughout the deposition, and the street is spelled "Mangum Street." Should you use "[*sic*]"?
  - No. It is not a direct quotation of a document.
  - This is likely a mispronounced word (Rule 84). If the mispronunciation is important, write the correct word in brackets after the first occurrence (Magnum [Mangum] Street). If the mispronunciation is not important, write the correct word in the transcript.

- Situation: The police report states, "Mr. Smith was seen fleeing the scene." Based on context, the report should state Mr. Jones. Should you use "[*sic*]"?
  - Yes, if you deem the error as an important error that may confuse the reader.
    - Transcript:  states, "Mr. Smith [*sic*] was
  - No, if you (1) deem the error as unimportant, (2) are unsure if the error is important, or (3) think the error is not likely to confuse the reader based on the context. Also, a witness or attorney should have corrected the error.


## Rule 125. A Word Written Phonetically

When a word is written phonetically in the transcript, add "[phonetic]" after the word.

- Q   What did Kathy have in her hand?
  A   It was some kind of gis-mo-gos-mo [phonetic].

- Q   What happened next?
  A   The dog ka-da-boomed [phonetic] on the floor.

- Q   What is Ryan's last name?
  A   It's Ka-lee-chaw [phonetic] or something like that.

These guidelines may be helpful in writing words phonetically:

- Use a hyphen between syllables.

- Use common words or syllables with easy-to-read pronunciations: be, eye, go, lay, man, so, tea.

- Writing a vowel sound at the end of a word can be problematic. Below are ideas for vowel spelling:

| Vowel | Short | Long |
|---|---|---|
| A | a, aw, ah | ay, ey |
| E | e, eh | e, ea, ee, ey, y |
| I | i, ih | ie, igh, y |
| O | o, oh | o, oa, oe, ow |
| U | u, uh | u, ew, oo, ou, ue |

See Rule 84 for mispronounced or made-up words.

# Punctuation Spacing

## Rule 126. Period or Question Mark

Use no space before and one space after a period or question mark. However, use no space after a period or question mark when followed by a closing parenthesis or closing quotation mark. Use no space before or after a decimal point.

- The bus had a flat tire. Did the children arrive at school on time? No, they did not. The bus arrived at 9:30 a.m.
- Lynn asked, "What time does the next ferry leave?"
- (Witness pointed to their right knee.)
- At the last weight loss meeting, I lost 2.3 pounds.

With a monospaced (`typewriter-like`) font, use two spaces after a period or question mark. Court reporting transcripts are more likely to use a monospaced font.

## Rule 127. Comma, Colon, or Semicolon

Generally, use no space before and one space after a comma, colon, or semicolon.

Use no space after a **comma**
- within a number ($1,000).
- when followed by a closing quotation mark.

Use no space after a **colon**
- with an expression of time (9:30 a.m.).
- with a ratio (2:3).
- between the volume and page number of a book series (*Computer Networks* 3:174).
- between the chapter and verse number of a Bible reference (Genesis 1:1).

With a monospaced (`typewriter-like`) font, use one space after a comma, colon, or semicolon. Traditionally, two spaces followed a colon in a monospaced font.

Examples:
- Before you mail the package, please stop at the bank and withdraw $1,000.
- "A ferry will cross the river in an hour," Lynn said.
- The children arrived at school around 9:30 a.m.; the bus had a flat tire.
- I dislike one thing: mean people.
- Mix the powder and water with a 1:3 ratio.
  - Spoken:  a one to three ratio.
  - Preferred:  a 1-to-3 ratio  (see Rule 184).
- The authors did not fully explain why they quoted Exodus 19:6 in *AI History* 2:41.

## Rule 128. Dash, Slash, or Hyphen

Use no space before or after a dash, slash, or hyphen. However, use one space after a suspending hyphen unless a comma follows (see Rule 107 examples), and use one space before and after a slash when an alternative is an open compound (see Rule 119 example).

- The punctuation videos are a win-win solution.
- He said, quote/unquote, "Get out."
- The affected nations—the U.S., Canada, and Mexico—signed the trade agreement.

With a monospaced (`typewriter-like`) font, write the dash as two connected hyphens with no space before and after the hyphens (`word--word`). Traditionally in court reporting, one space was used before and after the dash or connected hyphens to provide a better visual break.

## Rule 129. Quotation Marks, Parentheses, or Brackets

Use one space before and no space after an opening quotation mark, opening parenthesis, or opening bracket. Use no space before and one space after a closing quotation mark, closing parenthesis, or closing bracket.

However, use no space after a closing quotation mark, closing parenthesis, or closing bracket when another punctuation mark immediately follows.

- Did he really say, "I love you"?
- The eviction notice has an error: "sixty (30)" days.
- (Witness marked Exhibit 5.)
- Q   What is Ryan's last name?
  A   It's Ka-lee-chaw [phonetic] or something like that.


# Word Spelling

**Rule 130. Word Spelling**
Use the most recent edition of a Merriam-Webster dictionary for word spelling. The preferred dictionary is *Merriam-Webster's Collegiate Dictionary*.

If an alternate spelling is listed, the recommendation is to use the preferred or most common spelling. Use consistent spelling within a document or series of documents.

The four related Merriam-Webster dictionaries that may be used are:

- *Webster's Third New International Dictionary, Unabridged.*
  - This unabridged dictionary contains over 476,000 entries and was last updated in 2002.

- *Merriam-Webster's Collegiate Dictionary.*
  - This dictionary is an abridgment of *Webster's Third New International Dictionary, Unabridged*. The Eleventh Edition (2019 update) contains over 225,000 entries.
  - The collegiate dictionary is used by *The Gregg's Reference Manual*, *The Chicago Manual of Style*, and other popular style guides.

- *Merriam-Webster.com Dictionary.*
  - This free online dictionary contains about 240,000 entries and is regularly updated.

- *Merriam-Webster.com Unabridged*
  - This online unabridged dictionary is currently subscription based and contains about 490,000 entries. It is based on *Webster's Third New International Dictionary, Unabridged*.

# Italics

**Rule 131. Title of a Published, Produced, or Released Work**
Italicize the title of a published, produced, or released work, especially the title of a work consisting of smaller units (see below list). Do <u>not</u> italicize a software or video game title.

| | | | |
|---|---|---|---|
| book | movie | website | music album |
| magazine | TV series | blog | opera |
| newspaper | DVD | podcast series | play |
| journal | video | | musical |
| report | radio show | painting | ballet |
| pamphlet | speech | drawing | |
| | | photograph | |
| | | statue | |

- I published my first book, *The Court Reporter's Reference of Realtime Conflicts*, in November 2012.
- The article Mr. Sanchez quoted may be found in the *New York Times*, Section B, page 4.
- My favorite *Twilight Zone* episode is "To Serve Man."

See Rule 139 for the capitalization of a title or subtitle of a published, produced, or released work.

Use double quotation marks to enclose the title of a work within a larger work: book chapter, magazine article, newspaper article, song from an album, poem in a book, TV episode, web page, blog post, and so on (see Rule 82).


**Rule 132. Legal Citation**
The general format of a legal citation is the following:
- Italicize and capitalize the case names.
- Use an italicized "*v.*" to abbreviate the word *versus*.
- Do <u>not</u> italicize the following letters, numbers, words, and abbreviations that stand for the case, page, court, region, state, year, and so on.
  - However, italicize the reference words *ante*, *ibid.*, *id.*, *infra*, *post*, and *supra*.

Italicize and capitalize the case names in a short form of a legal citation.

- *United States v. Pepperman*, 976 F.2d 123 (3d Cir. 1992)
- *Ruben v. Shaffer*, 61 Cal.App.4<sup>th</sup> 213 (2003)
- *Bell Atlantic Corp. v. Twombly*, 550 U.S. 544, 553 (2007)
- *Roberts v. United States, supra*, 124 L.Ed.2d at p. 209.
- *Smith v. Shop-Rite*

## Rule 133. Unfamiliar Foreign Word or Phrase
Italicize an unfamiliar foreign word or phrase.

The best practice is <u>not</u> to italicize a foreign word or phrase listed in a Merriam-Webster dictionary. The court reporter may italicize any foreign word or phrase they deem "unfamiliar." Enclose any translation in double quotation marks (Rule 87).

- The editorial did not reflect the *vox populi.*

- *La citudad y los perros*, literally translated is "the city and the dogs," was published in 1963 with the title *The Time of the Hero.*

- Sally always felt like a *persona non grata* at her spouse's family gatherings.

- Scholars think the Prakrit word *majjao*, meaning "tom cat," derives from two earlier Sanskrit words.

It is <u>not</u> necessary to italicize the following legal words and phrases:

| | | |
|---|---|---|
| ad hoc | in extremis | per se |
| ad litem | in re | prima facie |
| a priori | in toto | postmortem |
| bona fide | ipsie dixit | pro bono |
| caveat emptor | ipso facto | pro forma |
| circa | magnum cum laude | pro rata |
| corpus delicti | mandamus | pro tempore |
| cum laude | mea culpa | quid pro quo |
| de facto | modus operandi | status quo |
| de jure | nom de plume | summa cum laude |
| ergo | non compos mentis | ultimatum |
| et al. | non sequitur | verbatim |
| ex officio | per annum | vice versa |
| fait accompli | per capita | vis-à-vis |
| habeas corpus | per diem | voir dire |

**Rule 134. Word Definition**
Italicize a word or phrase being defined, and enclose the
formal definition in double quotation marks (Rule 86).

- Sandra explained the meaning of the common Latin
  phrase *ad nauseam* using the dictionary definition: "to
  a sickening or excessive degree."
- The contract defines *monitoring* as "daily reviewing the
  location and reporting any hazards, damage, or
  deficiencies."
- The word *schedule* in the policy means "a list or
  inventory," not a date.


**Rule 135. Word Used as a Word**
Italicize a word used as a word or a lowercase letter used as a
lowercase letter.

Using italics shows the word itself is intended and not the
meaning of the word. Sometimes the word is introduced by the
phrase *the word*.

- Do not search for the word *punctuation* in this book.
- Though they sound the same, there is a difference
  between *premier* and *premiere*.
- Please mind your *p*'s and *q*'s.


**Rule 136. Gene and Scientific Name of a Plant or Animal**
Italicize a symbol or an abbreviation of a gene name. Also,
italicize the Latin name of a species and subspecies for plants
and animals.

Capitalize the Latin name of a plant or animal (see Rule 157).

Gene:
- Human genes include *IGH* (immunoglobulin heavy).
- *GIF* (gastric intrinsic factor) is a mouse gene.

Species and Subspecies:
A species name is a two-part name comprised of the capitalized genus name and the lowercase species name. Any abbreviation for the words *subspecies* or *variety* before a subspecies name (subsp., ssp., var., or f.) is not italicized.

- When Neanderthals (*Homo neanderthalensis*) split with modern humans (*Homo sapiens*) is unclear.
- *Natrix helvetica* became a separate species in 2017.
- *Schoenoplectus californicus* subsp. *Tatora* is a notable plant found on Lake Titicaca.

# Capitalization

**Rule 137. The Three Fundamental Capitalization Rules**
A proper noun is the official and complete name of a specific person, place, or thing. The three fundamental rules of capitalization are:

1. Capitalize a proper noun.
2. Capitalize an adjective derived from a proper noun.
3. Avoid capitalizing a short form of a proper noun. A short form may be capitalized when it represents the official and complete name AND distinction or emphasis is needed.

These three rules explain many of the following capitalization rules. The current trend in popular style guides, like *The Chicago Manual of Style*, is a preference for lowercase.

Person:
Capitalize a person's name or initials.

- Ward Stone Ireland
- William Shakespeare
- Napoleon Bonaparte
- J. R. R. Tolkien
  - Use a period and one space after an initial unless the name is only initials (JFK, LBJ).
- Catherine Zeta-Jones
  - Capitalize the names in a hyphenated last name.

For a participle in a name (de, d', de la, von), follow the source's capitalization. If the source is not available, follow a Merriam-Webster or biographical dictionary. A participle in a French, Spanish, or German name is frequently lowercase.

| | |
|---|---|
| Jean d'Alembert | French |
| Jean de La Fontaine | French |
| Manuel de Falla | Spanish |
| Manuel de Las Casas | Spanish |
| Ludwig von Humboldt | German |
| Johannes van Keere | Dutch |
| Luca Da Ponte | Italian |
| Tawfiq al-Hakim | Arabic |
| Mao Tse-tung | Chinese |
| Kim Jung-hee | Korean |

<u>Place</u>:
Capitalize the official and complete name of a specific place: continent, island, mountain, ocean, lake, river, world region, political division (country, state, county, province, territory, ward, precinct), city, town, village, building, structure, monument, park, public area, highway, street, and so on.

- Rocky Mountains; the Rockies
- Atlantic Ocean
- Mississippi River
- Australia; Down Under
- Japan
- New York City; the Big Apple
- Golden Gate Bridge
- Leaning Tower of Pisa
- South River Road

<u>Thing</u>:
Capitalize the official and complete name of a specific thing.

- Constitution of the United States; the Constitution
- The London Underground; the Underground; the Tube
- *The Age of Reason* by Thomas Paine
- The Enlightenment
- Microsoft Excel
  - Do not italicize a software title (Rule 131).
- iPad, iPhone, eBay
  - Do not capitalize lowercase proper nouns.

Adjective Derived From a Proper Noun:
- The best **Shakespearean** sonnets.
- Four delicious **Japanese** dumplings.
- A summary of the **Napoleonic** Wars.

## Rule 138. First Word After Punctuation

Capitalize the first word after a period or question mark. Do <u>not</u> capitalize the first word after a comma, semicolon, or dash unless it is the word *I*, a proper noun, or a proper adjective.

- Capitalize first words. Do not capitalize second words.
- Capitalize first words; do not capitalize second words.
- Should I capitalize all first words? No, not all.
- IPhone 13—did you have one?—was released in September 2021.
    - Capitalize a lowercase proper noun after a period or question mark. If possible, avoid beginning a sentence with a lowercase proper noun.

See Rule 48 for capitalization after a colon.

See Rule 73 for capitalization of a direct quotation.

## Rule 139. Title and Subtitle of a Published, Produced, or Released Work

Capitalize the title and subtitle of a published, produced, or released work using the following rules. Capitalize a hyphenated word as if the words were not hyphenated.

Capitalize the **first** word, the **last** word, and **all** words <u>except</u>
- articles (a, an, the).
- coordinating conjunctions (and, but, or, for, nor, so, yet).
- short prepositions (three or fewer letters) unless used adjectivally or adverbially (Hit the On Button, Turn Up the Volume).
- the word *to* in an infinitive (Nothing to See).
- Lowercase proper nouns (iPhone, eBay) unless it is the first word of a title or subtitle.

Use the above rules to capitalize the title of a heading, table, chart, graph, figure, or diagram in a document.

See Rule 82 for using double quotation marks with the title of a book chapter, magazine or newspaper article, and so on.

See Rule 131 for using italics with the title of a book, magazine, newspaper, movie, music album, and so on.

Examples:
- Marriage in the Middle Ages: A Comprehensive Guide
  - Insert a colon between a title and a subtitle.
- How to Buy the Best Real Estate Without Any Cash
- The Gentle Art of Forgiving and Forgetting
- How to Live Life With Both Feet off the Floor
- Sit Down and Listen: From On Button to Off Button
- A Review of Up-to-Date Computer Systems


## Rule 140. Title Before a Person's Name
Always capitalize a title before a person's name.

A title may be personal (Mr., Ms.), familial (Aunt, Uncle), executive (President, Director), professional (Dr., Professor), civic (Mayor, Governor), religious (Father, Reverend), or military related (General, Colonel).

- In early August 1992, Major John Smith led troops into combat for the first time.
- Did Mayor Margaret Clark speak at the fundraiser?
- I see the committee scheduled Rabbi Rosenfeld and Director Izzo for the next meeting.

Do <u>not</u> capitalize the following with a title:
- The words *acting, current, former*, or *late*.
- The prefix *ex-* or the suffix *-elect*.
  - Do <u>not</u> hyphenate *-elect* with an open compound: Vice President elect, County Assessor elect.

- Will acting Director Izzo address the committee?
- When will Mayor-elect Clark be sworn into office?

See Rule 193 for using the abbreviations Dr., Mr., Mrs., Ms., and Mx. before a person's name.


## Rule 141. Title After a Person's Name
A title after a person's name is usually not capitalized. Separate a title after a person's name with commas (see Rule 24 and Rule 26).

- Did Margaret Clark, mayor of the City of Menlo Park, speak at the fundraiser?
- I met Dianne Feinstein, senator from California, at a 2018 campaign rally.
- Albert Izzo, the director of finance, will attend the next committee meeting.

Identification Blocks:
Capitalize a title after a person's name in an identification block: signature block, front matter (transcript, report), addressee (envelope, letter, memo, message), and so on.

- Kalani Palakiko
  Chief, Project Management
- Albert Izzo
  Director of Finance

Nobility and High-Ranking Titles:
Nobility and high-ranking titles are no longer capitalized after a person's name. Traditionally, titles of nobility and of high-ranking international, national, and state officials were capitalized after a person's name including

- King, Queen, Pope, Prime Minister, President, and Vice President.
- Secretary of State, Attorney General, and other members of the U.S. presidential Cabinet.
- Senator, Representative, Chief Justice.
- Governor and Lieutenant Governor (of a state).

Document From an Organization:
A title after a person's name is frequently capitalized in a ceremonial or promotional document. Also, an organization (especially a government organization) normally capitalizes a title after a person's name when the title is related to the organization.

- Margaret Clark, Mayor of the City of Menlo Park, will speak at Saturday's fundraiser.
  - In a promotional document by the fundraiser.
- Dianne Feinstein, Senator from California, made a surprise visit to the Syracuse campaign rally.
  - In a Democratic Party newsletter.

**Rule 142. Title Substituted for a Person's Name**
Capitalize a title that substitutes for a person's name. This generally occurs in direct address (see Rule 22). Do <u>not</u> capitalize *sir*, *ma'am*, *madam*, or *miss*.

- Is it true that you stole city funds, Mayor?
- What time, Sergeant, did you arrive at the accident?
- My brother took Grandma out for dinner.
- Did Dad watch the baseball game last night?
- The Governor released the preliminary budget.
- Did the Senator vote against the bill?

**Rule 143. Family Relationship Title**
Capitalize a family relationship title before a person's name. Do not capitalize a title when it is preceded by a possessive pronoun: *my, your, his, her, our,* or *their*.

- When is Uncle Manuel returning from vacation?
- My brother took Grandma Sandra out for dinner.
- Did Aunt Julia drive her nephew to see a doctor?

**Rule 144. Name of a Business, Organization,
or Government Body**
Capitalize the official and complete name of a business, company, organization, association, foundation, institution, club, union, society, political party, university, college, school, or government body. Capitalize the official and complete name of any meeting, conference, or subdivision (board, committee, commission, department, or division).

Do not capitalize the generic use of *board, city, committee, company, council, county, court, department, federal, government, state,* or *union* (see Rule 145 and Rule 146).

<u>Short Form:</u>
Avoid capitalizing a short form. A short form may be capitalized when it represents the official and complete name AND distinction or emphasis is needed (Rule 137).

Businesses, organizations, or government bodies frequently capitalize short forms related to their business or organization in the documents they produce.

Capitalize the short form of an international or national-level judicial, legislative, or administrative body plus any major divisions including
- Cabinet (presidential); Supreme Court.
- Congress, House, Senate.
- the Administration (presidential, social security).
- the Bureau (budget, census, FBI).
- the Commission (communications, trade).
- the Department (state, justice, treasury).
- Parliament; the Crown.

<u>Business and Organization Examples</u>:
- The National Shorthand Reporters Association was founded in 1899. The association changed its name to the Nation Court Reporters Association in 1990.
  - In the second sentence, *association* may be capitalized in a document by the organization.

- Headquartered in Cupertino, California, Apple was founded in 1976 as Apple Computer Company.
  - Apple is the common name for Apple Inc., the company's official name since 2007.

- My mother is a Democrat; my father, a Republican.
  - Capitalize members of a political party.

- Alpha Delta Gamma women's fraternity is also known as Alpha Gam.

<u>Government Body Examples</u>:
- The Little Rock City Council added a new member to the Arts and Culture Commission.
- The Clark County Board of Supervisors meets Tuesdays and Wednesdays. The board meets Thursdays in a closed session for confidential matters.
  - In the second sentence, *board* may be capitalized in a document by Clark County.

- The gallery is open whenever the Senate is in session.
- The United States Census Bureau measures "America's people, places, and economy." The Bureau will release the 2010 census data in 2082.
  - In the second sentence, *bureau* is capitalized.

- Did Parliament adjourn until Monday morning?

**Rule 145. The Words *Federal* and *Government***
Do <u>not</u> capitalize the words *federal* or *government* unless it is part of a proper noun or is a party in the lawsuit.

- The government is corrupt.
- The federal government is assessing the situation.
- Did you read the Federal Bureau of Prisons report?
- The Government has not proven its case.
    - The government is a party in the lawsuit.


**Rule 146. The Words *City*, *County*, and *State***
Do <u>not</u> capitalize the words *city, county, or state* unless it is part of a proper noun or is a party in the lawsuit.

Should "New York City" be capitalized when the official name is the "City of New York"? Yes. Do <u>not</u> capitalize *city, county, or state* when it refers to a geographical location. However, capitalize *city, county, or state* whenever

- it is part of a noun. (The name of a city, county, or state precedes or follows the word *city, county, or state*.)

AND

- the noun refers to a government entity—namely, the ability to operate, regulate, or do business.

Examples:
- I was born in the city of Chicago.
    - Refers to a geographical location.
- Contact the City of Chicago for your birth certificate.
- The State of California passed a new law addressing the homeless crisis.
- Do state employees get 13 holidays a year?
- New York City prohibits the sale of fireworks.
- The city prohibits the sale of fireworks.
    - In a city document, the word *city* may be capitalized (see Rule 144).
- The burden of proof is on the State.
    - The state is a party in the lawsuit.

## Rule 147. Name of a Court or Grand Jury

Capitalize the official and complete name of a specific court or grand jury. Avoid capitalizing a short form. A short form may be capitalized when it represents the official and complete name AND distinction or emphasis is needed (Rule 137).

Do not capitalize the generic use of the words *court* or *grand jury*. Capitalize *court* when it refers to the U.S. Supreme Court or to the presiding judge.

- The Harris County Grand Jury will convene Tuesday.
- The grand jury will convene Tuesday.
- Only a superior court can rule on that issue.
- The case has been scheduled in Nevada County Superior Court, Department 17.
- That was a historic decision by the Court.
  - *Court* refers to the U.S. Supreme Court.
- The Court will issue a ruling tomorrow.
  - *Court* refers to the presiding judge.

## Rule 148. Court Officer

Only capitalize the title of a court officer (judge, bailiff, clerk) when used before a name or when the title substitutes for a person's name (see Rule 140 and Rule 142). Capitalize *Honor* when it refers to the presiding judge; do not capitalize any associated personal pronouns (his, her, your).

- Will Bailiff Jacobs please take Mr. Poke into custody.
- Does the clerk have a copy of the document?
- Which judge has the case? Is it Judge Mayhew?
- Q   Are you telling the truth? A judge will know.
  A   I'm sorry, Judge. I did, in fact, do it.
  Q   Well, your Honor, I rest my case.

## Rule 149. The Words *Plaintiff, Defendant,* and *Counsel*

Only capitalize the words *plaintiff*, *defendant*, or *counsel* when it substitutes for a party in the lawsuit (see Rule 142).

- Please get the Plaintiff from the hallway.
- The Court will allow the Defendant to continue.
- Are you telling me, Counsel, that you lost the diagram?
- In that case, the plaintiff sought punitive damages.
  - Use lowercase for other cases or cited authority.

**Rule 150. Court Documents**
Capitalize the official and complete title of a court document. A short form may be capitalized when it represents the official and complete name AND distinction or emphasis is needed (Rule 137).

Do not capitalize the generic use of the following words or phrases: *answers to interrogatories, contract, deed, deposition, exhibit, motion, notice of taking deposition, petition, request for production of documents, stipulation, will*, and so on.

- Is that Responses to Plaintiff's Second Set of Special Interrogatories, Question 47?
- Is that Special Interrogatories, Set 2, Question 47?
- Is Exhibit 12-E the email sent on December 12, 2022?
- Is that in the special interrogatories?
- Is that in the Special Interrogatories?
  - Distinction needed.

See Rule 81 for using quotation marks with a document title introduced by the words *marked*, *labeled*, or *titled*.

See Rule 114 for exhibit labeling (numbers preferred) and for using a hyphen between an exhibit label and a subpart.

**Rule 151. Brand, Product, Trademark, or Software Name**
Capitalize a brand, product, trademark, or software name. Follow the official spelling and style by consulting a Merriam-Webster dictionary or the company's website. If the name refers to the product in general, do not capitalize it.

- Can you use Microsoft Excel and Google Earth?
  - Do not italicize software titles (Rule 131).
- Because flu season is approaching, stock up on Robitussin, Tylenol, and Sudafed.
- Q  Did you have a thermos and Crest toothpaste?
  - *Thermos*, a brand name, is now a common term.
- A  Yes. They were in my Ford truck.

## Rule 152. Day, Month, Holiday, or Season

Capitalize the name of a day of the week or month of the year. Capitalize the name of a holiday, religious day, or any officially designated day. Do <u>not</u> capitalize season names.

- Is the staff meeting on Wednesday or Thursday?
- Never move to Phoenix in the middle of summer.
- William always confuses Memorial Day, which is in May, with Labor Day, which comes in September.

Holidays, Religious Days, and Designated Days Include:

| | | |
|---|---|---|
| April Fools' Day | Guy Fawkes Day | New Year's Eve |
| Ash Wednesday | Halloween | Palm Sunday |
| Ashura | Hanukkah | Passover |
| Boxing Day | Independence Day | Presidents' Day |
| Christmas Day | Juneteenth | Queen's Birthday |
| Christmas Eve | Kwanzaa | Ramadan |
| Cinco de Mayo | Labor Day | Remembrance Day |
| Columbus Day | Lent | Rosh Hashanah |
| Earth Day | Lincoln's Birthday | St. Patrick's Day |
| Easter Sunday | Martin Luther King | Thanksgiving Day |
| Election Day |   Jr. Day | Valentine's Day |
| Father's Day | Mawlid | Veterans Day |
| Flag Day | Memorial Day | Washington's |
| Fourth of July | Mother's Day |   Birthday |
| Good Friday | New Year's Day | Yom Kippur |
| Groundhog Day | | |

## Rule 153. Ethnic Group, Nationality, or Language

Capitalize the name of an ethnic group, racial group, nationality, or language.

- When was the first contact between Italians and the Chinese?

- Sandy described the thief as "a short Caucasian man speaking broken English."

- Franco said his new girlfriend is Asian American and speaks fluent Mandarin Chinese.
  - Write a compound nationality as an open compound.

A term used for an ethnic or racial group may change with time or may reflect a personal preference. Terms include *African American, Asian, Asian American, European American, Native American, Black, White, Caucasian, Hispanic, Latino, Latina, Latinx*, and so on. Capitalize these terms.

For current usage of ethnic or racial terms, consult "Race-Related Coverage" in *The Associated Press Stylebook* or "Racial and Ethnic Identity" (Section 5.7) in the *Publication Manual for the American Psychological Association*.


## Rule 154. Act, Bill, Code, Law, or Treaty

Capitalize the official and complete name of an act, bill, code, law, or treaty. Do not capitalize a generic use of the word *act, bill, code, law,* or *treaty.*

- The Americans with Disabilities Act became law in 1990 and prohibits discrimination based on disability.
- The First Amendment of the Constitution of the United States was ratified in December 1791.
  - Capitalize parts of the U.S. Constitution.
  - Use words, not figures, for U.S. Constitution amendments (Thirteenth, Twentieth).
- Was the treaty signed between Canada and the United States of America?
- California Assembly Bill 1597, which would increase penalties for shoplifting, did not pass in 2022.


## Rule 155. Historical Event, Age, or Era

Capitalize the name of a historical event, age, or era. Most terms for a decade, century, or period are not capitalized (also see Rule 189). Do <u>not</u> capitalize *digital age, information age, nuclear age,* or *space age.*

- Counterfeiting was an effective war tactic during the **Revolutionary War**.
- Thomas Paine wrote *The Age of Reason* during the **Enlightenment** in the late **eighteenth century**.
  - See Rule 178 for writing *eighteenth*, not 18th.
- The **Second Great Awakening** happened after the **colonial period** of the **Modern Era**.
- Who is playing in the **World Series**?
  - Capitalize the name of a sporting event.

**Rule 156. Movement or Government Program**
Capitalize the name of a movement or accepted title of a government program. Do not capitalize a short form unless distinction or emphasis is needed (see Rule 137).

- The New Deal focused on relief, recovery, and reform.
- The Social Security Act was passed in 1965.
- Medicare and Medicaid are parts of Social Security.
- I have not received my social security payment.
- Did Occupy Wall Street and Black Lives Matter use similar protest methods?


**Rule 157. Scientific or Medical Terms**
Capitalize the name of a celestial body, an official geologic term, or the Latin name of a plant or animal. For a medical term (disease, treatment, anatomical part), the best practice is to only capitalize a proper name or adjective in the term.

- The Crab Nebula is in the Perseus Arm of the Milky Way.
- The Pleistocene epoch ended about 12,000 years ago.
- The biopsy was negative for non-Hodgkin's lymphoma.
- The Eustachian tube is better known as the auditory tube.
- Alfred identified the plant as deergrass (*Trichophorum cespitosum*).

Earth, Sun, and Moon:
Generally, only capitalize *earth, sun,* or *moon* when the context contains another planet or celestial body.

- Julia has a down-to-earth personality.
- Both Earth and Mars have an atmosphere.

Plant and Animal Names:
Capitalize the Latin name of a plant or animal, and italicize the name of the species (see Rule 136). The best practice for a common name of a plant or animal is to only capitalize a proper name or adjective. Consult a dictionary.

Medical Terms:
Consult a medical reference for the spelling and capitalization of a disease, infection, disorder, therapy, treatment, procedure, anatomical part, and so on. The best practice for a medical term is to only capitalize a proper name or adjective.

**Rule 158. Religious Terms**
Capitalize the name of a religion, religious movement, religious adherent, or an adjective derived therefrom. Capitalize a reference to a supreme being; the name of a religious building or religious event (past or future); or a work regarded as sacred. Major theological concepts are often capitalized.

- The Church of the Nativity is a Catholic church.
- Being born in Utah, I was raised among Mormons and Christians.
- We can only estimate the population of Egypt at the time of the biblical Exodus.
- Do you believe in God or Allah as contained in the Bible or Qur'an?
  - The *Merriam-Webster.com Dictionary* spells the Muslim sacred work as Koran with acceptable variants of Quran or Qur'an. The *AP Stylebook* lists Quran (preferred spelling) or Koran. Islamic and Arabic scholars seem to prefer Qur'an.

**Rule 159. Military Terms**
Capitalize the name of a military force (army, navy, air force), company, squadron, battalion, regiment, fleet, and so on. Capitalize the name of a war, battle, or campaign. Capitalize the name of a military (or civilian) ship, train, automobile, aircraft, or spacecraft. (Note: Ship, aircraft, and spacecraft names were traditionally italicized.)

- The Continental Army and the Continental Navy were founded in 1775.
- In World War II, the Allies chiefly consisted of Great Britain, the United States, and the Soviet Union.
- Andrew Jackson commanded the United States Army at the Battle of New Orleans during the War of 1812.
- The USS Enterprise, CVN-65, is the most decorated ship in U.S. naval history.
- Most people can recognize the Boeing B-17 Flying Fortress used during World War II.
  - Use a hyphen between a letter and a number in an aircraft name.

## Rule 160. Academic Subject, Course Title, or Degree

Capitalize the name of a specific academic subject or course title. Capitalize an academic degree after a person's name. Do not capitalize a general subject area or degree. Do not capitalize *freshman, sophomore, junior*, or *senior*.

- Q   Melissa wants a master of arts degree. Is she taking any American history?
    - o   Capitalize a proper noun or adjective in a general subject area or degree.
- A   As a sophomore, she is enrolled in History 104 and History 105.
- Q   Is Joan Herbert, Doctor of History, teaching those?
    - o   See Rule 24 for comma usage.
- A   Yes. She always teaches the fall semester classes.

## Rule 161. Award, Certificate, Honor, or Medal

Capitalize the name of a specific award, certificate, honor, or medal.

- Who won the Nobel Peace Prize in 1985?
- *Gone with the Wind* won the Academy Award in 1939.
- I have the Online Security Systems Certificate.

## Rule 162. Musical Key

Capitalize the letter of a musical key. Use a hyphen with the words *flat* or *sharp*. Consult a musical reference.

- Haydn's symphony is in A minor, not A-sharp minor.
- The concerto is in B-sharp, not C major.
- Bach's famous fugue is in D minor, not D-flat minor.

## Rule 163. The Words *North, South, East*, and *West*

Capitalize *north, south, east, west, northeast*, and so on when it refers to a specific geographical area. Do <u>not</u> capitalize these words when they refer to a direction or general location.

- I moved from the East Coast to the South in 2018.
- Ms. Anderson is a respected lawyer in the Midwest.
- The car traveled north on Michigan Street.
- My work office is 30 minutes northeast of my home.
- How many Amish communities are in northern Ohio?

# Numbers

## Rule 164. Using Words Vs. Figures

Use words for the numbers zero to ten (0 to 10), and use figures for the numbers above ten. Exceptions include using figures to express a date, time (except with *o'clock*), monetary amount, address, ordinal, technical measurement, percentage, fraction, decimal fraction, numbered reference, and so on (see below sections and Rule 165 to Rule 191).

- Mr. Smith bought three turkeys for Thanksgiving.
- Ms. Anderson has 63 pairs of shoes.
- I live at 408 Fifth Avenue.
- Fifty-eight runners competed in the ultramarathon.
- I bought several hundred acres of land.
  - Use words for indefinite amounts.

<u>Using Words for a Number Over Ten:</u>
A number over ten may be expressed in words when (1) no rule requires expression as a figure AND (2) the number can be expressed in one or two words (a hyphenated word, like twenty-one, counts as one word) AND (3) de-emphasis of the number is desired. Avoid if the usage is not intentional.

<u>Using a Figure for a Number Between Zero and Ten:</u>
A number between zero and ten may be expressed as a figure to aid rapid reading or to emphasize the number. Avoid if the usage is not intentional.

<u>Zero Expressed by the Words *Oh, Aught,* or *Nil*:</u>
A speaker may express the number zero with the word *oh, aught,* or *nil.* When the word means zero and zero should be expressed in words, use the word spoken. When it should be expressed as a figure, use the figure 0.

<u>Figure Style vs. Word Style:</u>
Court reporting uses "Figure Style" to write numbers. Figure Style focuses on using words for the numbers one to ten and using figures for numbers above ten. "Word Style" focuses on using words for numbers that can be expressed in one or two words (a hyphenated word, like twenty-one, counts as one word) and using figures for other numbers. Both styles have the same or similar exceptions for using figures to express a date, time, monetary amount, and so on.

*The Chicago Manual of Style* contains and *The Associated Press Stylebook* specifies a Figure Style that uses words for single-digit numbers (one to nine) and uses figures for ten and above. They have similar exceptions for using figures to express a date, time, monetary amount, and so on.


## Rule 165. Hyphen in a Spelled-Out Number

Use a hyphen to spell a number between 21 (twenty-one) and 99 (ninety-nine). Do not use a hyphen to spell the portion of a number over one hundred.

The examples show how to express a number with words. These numbers would normally be expressed with figures.

- Did you say thirty-seven or seventy-three?
- I paid forty-five hundred for the used car.
- The U.S. national debt is over thirty-one trillion dollars.
- The population of the town has ranged between five hundred and three thousand.

- 537:   five hundred thirty-seven
- 2468:   two thousand four hundred sixty-eight
- 6181:   six thousand one hundred eighty-one


## Rule 166. Comma Separator in a Figure

Use a comma to separate thousands, millions, billions, trillions, and so on. Do not use comma separators with a year, page number, line number, house/building number, ZIP code, telephone number, room number, or an acoustic or broadcast frequency (2000 Hz).

- Nick lives at 9112 Plymouth Avenue.
- The population was 1,087 in 1732; it grew to 25,304 in 1832; and it exploded to 1,415,439 in 1932.
- Sophia's statement that she left the company in 2015 is found on page 1024, line 17, of her deposition.

A serial number (order, invoice, parcel, and so on) typically does not contain comma separators. However, it may contain other separators, like hyphens or spaces.

- Order 55038 was shipped on August 24.
- Is the assessor's parcel number 016-0944-010?
- His social security number is 999-00-1111.
  - See Rule 188 for social security numbers.

## Rule 167. Consistent Format for Related Numbers

Use a consistent format for related numbers in the same context. Use figures for related numbers when one number would be expressed in words and the other number would be expressed in figures.

- I own **three** horses, and they eat about **12** bales of hay each week.
  - The numbers are not related.
- I own **12** chickens and **3** dogs.
  - The numbers are related.
- Q  How many items did you order that morning?
  A  I ordered **5** things.
  Q  Anything that evening?
  A  Yes, **15**.

## Rule 168. Number Precedes *Million, Billion*, or *Trillion*

When a number or monetary amount precedes the word *million, billion,* or *trillion,* use a figure for the number when the number is a whole number (1 million) or a whole number with one decimal place (1.2 million). Use a consistent format for related numbers (Rule 167).

- The worldwide human population is 7.7 billion.
- The YouTube video had 1.2 million views last week.
- Is $31 trillion the current U.S. national debt?
- The company's annual revenue is $5 million.
- The 2020 labor cost was $950,000. In 2021 it was $1,200,000.
  - Not: "$950,000" and "$1.2 million" (consistent format is required).

## Rule 169. Number at the Beginning of a Sentence

For a number at the beginning of a sentence, use words when the number can be expressed in one or two words. Use figures when the number would be expressed in three or more words. A hyphenated word, like twenty-one, counts as one word.

- Twenty-one cows escaped through a hole in the fence.
- Three thousand people signed the pledge.
- 214 cows escaped through a hole in the fence.
  - "Two hundred fourteen" is three words.
- 126 of the 151 applicants had work experience.
  - "One hundred twenty-six" is three words.
- Q   What is the apartment number?
  A   73A.
  - Do not use words to express a number containing both numbers and letters (an alphanumeric number).

In formal writing, a number at the beginning of a sentence is always expressed in words; and the sentence would be rephrased when the number cannot be expressed in one or two words. Because court reporters cannot rephrase the words of a transcript, using figures for a number at the beginning of a sentence will be allowed.

## Rule 170. Plural of a Figure

Form the plural of a figure by adding *s*.

- Tonight's low temperature will be in the 20s.
- Computer proliferation exploded in the 1980s.
- Madison's ZIP code contains two 5s.

## Rule 171. Date Formatting

Use figures to express the year and the day of the month in a date. See the following formatting sections for comma usage and placement.

Use a closing apostrophe mark (') when the first two digits of a year are omitted (see Rule 101).

Do <u>not</u> abbreviate the name of the month or the day of the week unless space is limited, like a list or table. Use the first three letters of the word with no period (Jan, Sep, Mon, Thu).

Format: *Month Day, Year*
Place a comma after the day of the month. Place a comma after the year if midsentence.
- My son was born on April 5, 2013.
- I went on June 18, 2018, to see the doctor.

Format: *DayOfTheWeek, Month Day, Year*
Place a comma after the day of the week and the day of the month. Place a comma after the year if midsentence.
- My son was born on Saturday, April 5, 2013.
- I went on Monday, June 18, 2018, to see the doctor.

Format: *Day Month Year*
No comma between date elements. This format is widely used outside the United States, It is also used in the U.S. military, in some academic fields, and with genealogical databases.
- My son was born on 5 April 2013.
- I went on 18 June 2018 to see the doctor.

Format: *Month Year*
No comma between the month and the year.
- My son was born in April 2013.
- I went in June 2018 to see the doctor.
- The historic storms occurred in January '23.
  - Spoken:  January twenty-three  (see Rule 101).

Format: *Month Day*
No comma between the month and the day of the month.
- My son was born on April 5.
- I went on June 18 to see the doctor.

Date Expressed Using All Numbers:
Use figures separated with slashes when a date is expressed entirely with numbers. If the speaker uses a different punctuation mark between the figures, use the spoken punctuation mark. However, use a hyphen if "dash" is said.
- My son was born on 4/5/2013.
  - Spoken:  four, five, two thousand thirteen.
- We moved to Albia, New York, on 8/12/'03.
  - Spoken:  eight, twelve, oh three.
- I went on 6-18-2018 to see the doctor.
  - Spoken:  six, dash, eighteen, dash, two thousand eighteen.

<u>Day Expressed as an Ordinal</u>:
Though the day is spoken as an ordinal (1st, 2nd, 3rd), it is written as a cardinal number (1, 2, 3). Only write an ordinal when the speaker uses an isolated ordinal for the day or uses an ordinal before the month. Write *st, nd, rd*, or *th* on the line, not superscript (Rule 178).

- I went on June 18, 2018, to see the doctor.
  - Spoken:  June 18th, 2018.
- My client did not receive the notice dated the 3rd.
- My son was born on the 5th of April.

## Rule 172. Time Before A.M. or P.M.

Use figures to express time before *a.m.* or *p.m.* Place a colon between the hour and minutes, and use lowercase letters with periods and no spaces (*a.m.* or *p.m.*).

- I leave for work at 7:30 a.m.
- At 5:17 p.m., I arrived at the scene.
- Debbie gets up at 4:45 a.m. every day.

<u>Time on the Hour</u>:
For a time on the hour, the best practice is to include the colon and zeros. Omitting the colon and zeros is acceptable unless a related time in the context requires a consistent format.

- The ferry leaves at 7:00 a.m.
  - Acceptable:  7 a.m.
- Did you say 9:00 p.m.?
  - Acceptable:  9 p.m.
- A ferry leaves at 7:00 a.m. and 7:30 a.m.
  - Not:  7 a.m.  (consistent format required).
- Did you say 9:00 a.m. or 9:10 a.m.?
  - Not:  9 a.m.  (consistent format required).

## Rule 173. Time in Hours and Minutes (Without A.M. or P.M.)

For a time expressed without *a.m.* or *p.m.*, the best practice is to use figures with a colon between the hour and minutes.

- I leave for work at 7:30.
  - Spoken:  seven-thirty.
- Debbie gets up at 4:45 every day.
  - Spoken:  four forty-five.

<u>Time on the Hour</u>:
For a time on the hour, the best practice is to use a figure with
a colon and zeros. Using a word is acceptable unless a related
time in the context requires a consistent format.

- The ferry leaves at 7:00.
  - Acceptable:  seven.
- Did you say 9:00?
  - Acceptable:  nine.
- A ferry leaves at 7:00 and 7:30.
  - Spoken:  seven and seven-thirty.
  - Not:  seven and 7:30  (consistent format required).
- Did you say 9:00 or 9:10?
  - Spoken:  nine and nine-ten.
  - Not:  nine or 9:10  (consistent format required).

## Rule 174. Time With O'clock

For a time on the hour before *o'clock* (most cases), the best
practice is to use words. Using figures without a colon and
zeros is acceptable. When a time in hour and minutes
precedes *o'clock*, use words.

- The meeting started at five o'clock.
  - Acceptable:  5 o'clock
  - Not:  5:00 o'clock
- Did you leave for work at seven o'clock in the morning?
  - Acceptable:  7 o'clock
  - Not:  7:00 o'clock
- The meeting started at four-thirty o'clock.
  - Not:  4:30 o'clock

## Rule 175. Military Time

Express military time as a four-digit number without a colon
between the hour and minutes.

- The ferry leaves at 0700 hours.
  - Spoken:  "zero, seven hundred" or "seven hundred."
  - Military time 0700 hours is 7 a.m.
- At 1730 hours, I took dinner in the mess hall.
  - Spoken:  seventeen-thirty hours
  - Military time 1730 hours is 5:30 p.m.

**Rule 176. Monetary Amounts**
Use figures to express a monetary amount. Only write the dollar sign ($) when the word *dollar* is said.

- Each can of soup costs $2.95.
  - Spoken:  two dollars and ninety-five cents.
- The wedding dress costs $2,337.49.
  - Spoken:  two thousand three hundred thirty-seven dollars and forty-nine cents.
- Inflation just raised the price by 1.20 to $16.44
  - Spoken:  by one-twenty to sixteen dollars and forty-four cents.


Even Monetary Amount:
For an even monetary amount, do <u>not</u> write the decimal point and zeros unless a related monetary amount in the context requires a consistent format.

- My rent is $800 per month.
  - Spoken:  eight hundred dollars.
- Ms. Anderson paid $45,000 for the sedan.
  - Spoken:  forty-five thousand dollars
- Ms. Anderson paid 45,000 for the sedan.
  - Spoken:  forty-five thousand
- The pens ranged from $2.00 to 3.50.
  - Spoken:  two dollars to three-fifty.
  - Consistent format required


Amount Under One Dollar:
For an amount under a dollar, write *cents* when the amount stands by itself. Write a dollar sign with a zero before the decimal point when it is used with another amount over one dollar because the context requires a consistent format.

- A can of tomato sauce costs 77 cents.
  - Spoken:  seventy-seven cents
- A can of chicken soup is $0.89, and a four-pack costs only $2.95.
  - Spoken:  "eight-nine cents" and "two dollars and ninety-five cents."
  - Consistent format required.

## Rule 177. Address Formatting

Use figures to express the house/building number and ZIP code in an address. Use the word *One* instead of the figure *1* for the house/building number when readability is improved. See the below sections for using commas to separate address elements.

- I live at 4550 Live Oak Way.
- Taylor lives at 834 Main Street.
- Francis lives at 1 Live Oak Way.
  - Or: One Live Oak Way

<u>Numbered Streets</u>:

For a numbered street, the best practice is to follow Rule 178 (use words for first to tenth; use figures for above tenth). Using the word or figure format that appears on the location's street name sign is acceptable.

- I do not live at 914 Third Avenue.

- Taylor does not live at One 13th Street.
  - Not: 1 13th Avenue

- Who lives at 3030 24th Avenue?

- Sandy lives at 6109 Forty-Fourth Avenue.
  - "Forty-Fourth" is on the location's street name sign.
  - Recommend: 44th Avenue

<u>Envelope Format</u>:

*First Line*: Place the house/building number and street name on the first line without a comma between them. Any apartment or room number follows separated by a comma.

*Second Line*: Place the city, state, and ZIP code on the second line. Only place a comma between the city and state.

Do not use a comma separator with a house/building number or a ZIP code (Rule 166).

- 914 Third Street
  Kirtland, Ohio 44024

- 220 Cornwall Road, Apartment 42
  Woodside, California 94062

- 5162 East 13th Avenue
  New York, New York 10012

<u>Within-a-Sentence Format</u>:
Use "Envelope Format" with a comma instead of the line break between the first and second lines. Place a comma after the ZIP code when the address is midsentence.

- My address is 914 Third Street, Kirtland, Ohio 44024.

- Please use 220 Cornwall Road, Apartment 42, Woodside, California 94062, for all correspondence.

- Is 5162 East 13th Avenue, New York, New York 10012, your current address?

<u>Within-a-Sentence Format With Omitted Elements</u>:
Use "Within-a-Sentence Format" for the included address elements. Place a comma after the following (if included): the street name, an apartment or room number, the city, the ZIP code, and the state if no ZIP code.

- I live on Third Street, Kirtland, Ohio.

- Are you receiving mail at the 220 Cornwall Road, Apartment 42, address?

- Please use my address on 13th Avenue, New York, for all future correspondence.

<u>Abbreviations</u>:
In an address, do <u>not</u> abbreviate *Avenue, Street, North, East, Room*, and so on unless space is limited, like a list or table. An abbreviation on a mailing envelope is acceptable.

| <u>Word</u> | <u>Abbrev.</u> | <u>Word</u> | <u>Abbrev.</u> |
|---|---|---|---|
| Avenue | Ave. | Lane | Ln. |
| Boulevard | Blvd. | Parkway | Pkwy. |
| Court | Ct. | Place | Pl. |
| Drive | Dr. | Post Office Box | P.O. Box |
| Expressway | Expy. | Road | Rd. |
| Highway | Hwy. | Street | St. |
| North | N. | South | S. |
| East | E. | West | W. |
| Apartment | Apt. | Room | Rm. |
| Building | Bldg. | Suite | Ste. |

U.S. State Abbreviations:

Do not abbreviate the state name in an address unless space is limited, like a list or table. However, use an abbreviation for the state name on a mailing envelope.

| State | Abbrev. | State | Abbrev. |
|-------|---------|-------|---------|
| Alabama | AL | Nebraska | NE |
| Alaska | AK | Nevada | NV |
| Arizona | AZ | New Hampshire | NH |
| Arkansas | AR | New Jersey | NJ |
| California | CA | New Mexico | NM |
| Colorado | CO | New York | NY |
| Connecticut | CT | North Carolina | NC |
| Delaware | DE | North Dakota | ND |
| Florida | FL | Ohio | OH |
| Georgia | GA | Oklahoma | OK |
| Hawaii | HI | Oregon | OR |
| Idaho | ID | Pennsylvania | PA |
| Illinois | IL | Rhode Island | RI |
| Indiana | IN | South Carolina | SC |
| Iowa | IA | South Dakota | SD |
| Kansas | KS | Tennessee | TN |
| Kentucky | KY | Texas | TX |
| Louisiana | LA | Utah | UT |
| Maine | ME | Vermont | VT |
| Maryland | MD | Virginia | VA |
| Massachusetts | MA | Washington | WA |
| Michigan | MI | Washington, DC | DC |
| Minnesota | MN | West Virginia | WV |
| Mississippi | MS | Wisconsin | WI |
| Missouri | MO | Wyoming | WY |
| Montana | MT | | |

Limited Space Examples:

- 914 Third St.
- 220 Cornwall Rd., Apt. 42
- 5162 E. 13th Ave.

Mailing Envelope Format Examples:

- 914 Third Street
  Kirtland, OH 44024

- 220 Cornwall Road, Apartment 42
  Woodside, CA 94062

**Rule 178. Ordinals**
Use words for the ordinals first to tenth, and use figures for the ordinals above tenth (third, seventh, 11th, 23rd). Write *st, nd, rd,* and *th* on the line, not superscript. Use figures for related ordinals where one ordinal would use words and the other ordinal would use figures.

- Isabella won second place at the spelling bee.
- Her brother finished 12th in the competition.
- Chris, a novice runner, placed 92nd in the marathon.
- In 2020, Nick ranked 6th statewide. In 2021, he dropped to 14th.
    - Not:  sixth  (consistent format required).

Confusion about using words versus figures for ordinals comes from the difference between Word Style and Figure Style (see Rule 164 for description). Word Style, used by many books and academic works, uses words for first through one hundredth and figures above one hundredth. Figure Style, used mostly in newspapers and business documents, uses words for first to tenth and figures above tenth.

See Rule 154 for using words, not figures, for amendments to the U.S. Constitution.

See Rule 171 for using ordinals with dates.

See Rule 177 for numbered streets.

<u>Century, Birthday, Anniversary, and Grade Level</u>:
Use words for an ordinal regarding a century. Use words for an ordinal regarding a birthday, anniversary, or school grade level; however, following Rule 178 is acceptable.

- The *Age of Reason* was written during the late eighteenth century.
    - Not:  18th century

- We will celebrate our twenty-fifth wedding anniversary this Saturday.
    - Acceptable:  25th
- Is Sierra in the eleventh or twelfth grade?
    - Acceptable:  11th or 12th

**Rule 179. Technical Measurements**
Use figures to express a technical measurement, such as length, width, area, weight, volume, distance, time, temperature, or a person's age. When a measurement does not have a technical significance, follow Rule 164 (words for zero to ten and figures for above ten).

Do <u>not</u> separate parts of a measurement with punctuation (6 pounds 2 ounces). Unless space is limited (like a list or table), do <u>not</u> abbreviate *inches, feet, pounds, ounces, degrees*, and so on. Do <u>not</u> use an "x" to write the words *by* or *times*.

- Ethan's drive time to New York: 1 hour 7 minutes.
  - Not:  1 hour, 7 minutes
- With all the traffic caused by the accident, it took me two hours to drive to work.
  - Not:  2 hours  (likely no technical significance)
- Clara is 12 years 8 months.
  - Not:  12 years, 8 months
- The hole measured 3 by 5 inches.
  - Not:  3 x 5 inches
- The freezer operates between 30 and 36 degrees Fahrenheit.
  - Capitalize *Fahrenheit* and *Celsius*.
- The team is strictly for 8-year-old boys.
  - Not:  eight-year-old
- My five-year-old daughter twirled in her dress
  - Or:  5-year-old  (if technical significance)

When the unit of measure is missing (inches, feet, pounds), the best practice is to write the number with words.

- The freezer is set at thirty-two.
- My nephew is six, seven.
  - See Rule 185 for writing adjacent numbers.

When a technical measurement is used as an adjective, hyphenate the elements (see Rule 109 and Rule 110).

- The two-hour drive to work was all traffic.
- My 6-foot-7-inch nephew plays on the varsity team.
- Did you see the 3-by-5-inch hole?

## Rule 180. Percentages

Use figures with the word *percent* to express a percentage with technical significance (most cases). If there is no technical significance, use words when the number can be expressed in one or two words; use figures otherwise.

Do <u>not</u> use the percent symbol (%) unless space is limited, like a list or table. If the percentage is less than one, use a zero before the decimal point.

- Students averaged 82 percent on the midterm.
- Annual growth rates varied between 2.2 and 4.7 percent.
- The inflation rate in 2017 was 0.8 percent.
- You are one hundred percent correct.
  - No technical significance.


## Rule 181. Fractions

Use words to express a fraction unless it is (1) a "long" fraction, (2) a technical measurement, or (3) part of a mixed number.

A "simple" fraction has the format of a single-digit numerator over a single-digit denominator: 1/2, 3/4, 8/9. A "long" fraction is any fraction that is not a simple fraction: 3/10, 5/16, 17/32.

Hyphenate a fraction expressed in words: two-thirds, three-fourths, eight-ninths. For a fraction expressed in figures, use a slash (/) with no space before and after the slash (1/4). For a mixed number, insert one space between the whole number the and fraction (3 1/4); do not insert a hyphen.

- We need a two-thirds majority for approval.

- Is one-fourth of the U.S. population obese?

- The tank level is about two-thirds full.
  - Use "2/3 full" for a technical measurement.

- The report showed 11/40 of the focus group initially selected the product.
  - Fraction is a "long" fraction.

- The width of the crack is 3/8 of an inch.
  - Fraction is a technical measurement.
  - Not:  three-eights

- Her infant is 4 1/2 months old.
  - Fraction is part of a mixed number.
  - Not:  4-1/2

Use words to express the phrases *a half* and *a quarter*.

- I never let my car drop below a quarter tank.
- Did someone eat a half of the cookies?

**Rule 182. Decimal Fractions**
Use figures to express a decimal fraction. Use a zero before the decimal point for an amount less than one (0.4). However, do not use a zero before the decimal point when the number cannot be greater than one: gun caliber, batting average, and some statistical values.

- At the last weight-loss meeting, I lost 2.2 pounds.
- A modern marathon is 26.22 miles.
- We found the murder weapon: a Colt .45 handgun.
- The instructions in boldface state to slowly add 0.35 grams of magnesium.
  - Spoken: "zero point three five" or "point three five."

When an exhibit contains a decimal fraction and the speaker uses a fraction (often stated in the *hundredths* or *thousandths*), write it as a decimal fraction.

- The instructions in boldface state to slowly add 0.35 grams of magnesium.
  - Spoken: "thirty-five hundredths"

**Rule 183. Numbered References**
Use a figure to express a numbered reference. Capitalize all reference words except the words *page, paragraph, sentence, line, verse, note, size*, and *step*.

Separate numbered references with commas. Abbreviate *number* as "No." and *numbers* as "Nos." when used between the reference word and the numbered reference.

- I love Act 2, Scene 7, of Shakespeare's *As You Like It*.
- Mr. Smith's testimony starts on page 5, line 10, of the deposition dated September 19, 2019.
- The ordinance language the council member quoted is Chapter 1, Section 108, paragraph 2, sentence 5.
- Whose name is on Policy No. 2304997?

**Rule 184. Ratios, Scores, Voting Results, and Mathematics**
Use figures to express a number in a ratio, proportion, betting odd, voting result, sports score or standing, or mathematical expression. Hyphenate the elements when they are used as an adjective (see Rule 109 and Rule 110).

Ratio:
- A ratio of 5 to 2.
- A 5-to-2 ratio.

Proportion:
- A proportion of powder and water of 1 to 3.
- Use 1 part powder to 3 parts water.

Odds:
- The odds were 100 to 1.
- A 100-to-1 chance.

Voting Results:
- A vote of 18 to 9.
- An 18-to-9 vote.
  - Also acceptable: An 18-9 vote.

Sporting Score or Standing:
- The team lost 4 to 3.
- The team now has a 12-4-2 record.

Mathematical Expression:
- Divide by 12 to find the average.
- Please multiply that by 7 and then add 100.


**Rule 185. Adjacent Numbers**
When two adjacent numbers are both expressed in words or figures, separated them with a comma.

When two adjacent numbers are part of a compound modifier (both numbers collectively describe the noun), use words for the first number and figures for the second number unless the second number would be much shorter if expressed in words.

<u>Both Numbers Expressed in Words or Numbers</u>:
- In 2017 three students failed the final exam.
  - No comma is necessary because both numbers (2017, three) are not expressed in words or figures.
  - See Rule 7 for comma usage.
- In 2017, 52 students failed the final exam.
- For Account No. 933216, $800 was charged in March.
- My nephew is six, seven.
- Did Linda say for the staff meeting at three, eight people will attend?
  - Recommend:  at 3:00 eight people  (Rule 173)

<u>Compound Modifier</u>:
- Liam received twelve $50 gift cards for his birthday.
- Maggie owns two 4-bedroom homes.
- Kaitlyn found 150 ten-dollar bills in a paper bag.
- Aidan needs 525 two-page leaflets printed.


**Rule 186. Page or Year Range**

An en dash (–) with no space before or after the character <u>may</u> be used to show a page or year range. Using a hyphen is also acceptable but should be avoided. Use an en dash when the word *to* separates the two figures. Do <u>not</u> use an en dash when (1) there are omitted figures or (2) when the words *from* or *between* introduce the number range.

- A severe drought occurred from 1928 to 1935.

- The cost analysis is on pages 158–165.
  - Spoken:  pages 158 to 165.
  - Also correct:  158 to 165.
  - Acceptable but avoid (hyphen):  158-165.

- During 2015–2017, Francis headed the department.
  - Spoken:  during 2015 to 2017.
  - Also correct:  2015 to 2017.
  - Acceptable but avoid (hyphen):  2015-2017.

- During 2015 to '17, Francis headed the department.
  - Spoken:  during 2015 to 17.
  - Not:  2015–'17  (also not with hyphen: 2015-'17)
  - See Rule 101 for apostrophe usage.

A slash <u>may</u> be used between consecutive years to indicate the last part of the first year and the first part of the second year. An en dash is typically used, and a hyphen is also acceptable but should be avoided.

- Did you see the expenses for fiscal year 2019/2020?
    - Typically written (en dash):  2019–2020.
    - Acceptable but avoid (hyphen):  2019-2020.

- For 2022/'23, costs when up 6 percent.
    - Spoken:  2022 twenty-three.
    - Typically written (en dash):  2022–'23.
    - Acceptable but avoid (hyphen):  2022-'23.

## Rule 187. Telephone Number

Use figures to express a telephone number, and use hyphens to separate the parts of a telephone number. In the United States and Canada, a telephone number consists of a three-digit area code, a three-digit exchange prefix, and a four-digit line number. When an extension is given after a telephone number, capitalize *Extension* and separate it with a comma.

- My work number is 489-555-3073, and my cell phone is 312-555-2839.

- Q   Is your phone number 777-555-4433?
  A   No. It's 777-555-4343, Extension 321.

Previously, enclosing the area code in parentheses was acceptable because dialing it was not necessary for a local call. Now that many locations require the area code for a local call, do not enclose it in parentheses.

## Rule 188. Social Security Number

Use figures to express a social security number, and use hyphens to separate the parts of a social security number (three digits, two digits, then four digits).

- His social security number is 999-00-1111.

- Q   I'm trying to read your handwriting. Is your social security number 777-00-9999?
  A   No. It's 111-00-9999. My 1s look like 7s.

**Rule 189. Decades and Centuries**
Use figures to express a decade. Use words to express a century spoken as an ordinal (nineteenth century), but use figures to express a century spoken with the word *hundreds* ("1900s" when "nineteen hundreds" is spoken).

- My parents divorced in the late 1980s or early 1990s.
  - Spoken: late nineteen eighties or early nineteen nineties.
- My parents divorced in the late '80s or early '90s.
  - Spoken: late eighties or early nineties.
  - See Rule 101 for an apostrophe with omitted figures.
- Thomas Paine was born in the eighteenth century.
  - Most centuries are not capitalized (Rule 155).
- Thomas Paine was born in the 1700s.
  - Spoken: seventeen hundreds.
- Why are the 1900s called the twentieth century?
  - Spoken: nineteen hundreds called the twentieth century.

**Rule 190. Roman Numerals**
Use a roman numeral when the phrase *roman numeral* precedes the number. Use a roman numeral with reference to a U.S. Constitution article or amendment or reference to a state constitution.

- Is that Section VI of the agreement?
  - Spoken: section roman numeral six
- The quote is in Volume III, Chapter XXIX.
  - Spoken: volume roman numeral three, chapter roman numeral twenty-nine.
- Article II, Section 2, of the U.S. Constitution states the President is the "Commander in Chief of the Army."
  - Spoken: article two, section two
- That statistic is in the report preface on page iv.
  - Spoken: page roman numeral four.
  - Pages of a preface or table of contents in a book or report use lowercase roman numerals: i, ii, iii, iv.

Roman Numeral Table:

| Number | Roman Numeral | Number | Roman Numeral | Number | Roman Numeral |
|---|---|---|---|---|---|
| 1 | I | 16 | XVI | 80 | LXXX |
| 2 | II | 17 | XVII | 90 | XC |
| 3 | III | 18 | XVIII | 100 | C |
| 4 | IV | 19 | XIX | 200 | CC |
| 5 | V | 20 | XX | 300 | CCC |
| 6 | VI | 21 | XXI | 400 | CD |
| 7 | VII | 22 | XXII | 500 | D |
| 8 | VIII | 23 | XXIII | 600 | DC |
| 9 | IX | 24 | XXIV | 700 | DCC |
| 10 | X | 25 | XXV | 800 | DCCC |
| 11 | XI | 30 | XXX | 900 | CM |
| 12 | XII | 40 | XL | 1000 | M |
| 13 | XIII | 50 | L | 2000 | MM |
| 14 | XIV | 60 | LX | 3000 | MMM |
| 15 | XV | 70 | LXX | | |

## Rule 191. Numbers With the Words *Odd, Some, Some-Odd* and *Something*

Hyphenate a figure with the suffix *odd*, *some*, *some-odd*, or *something*. Using words instead of a figure is acceptable for a number with no technical significance (see Rule 179).

- The set contains 40-odd metal tools.
  - Acceptable:  forty-odd.
- Abby spent 20-some hours practicing for the test.
  - Acceptable: twenty-some.
- I was told 50-some-odd people attended the party.
  - Acceptable: fifty-some-odd.
- Was the car going 70-something miles per hour?

# Abbreviation

## Rule 192. Guidelines and Some Common Abbreviations

Check a Merriam-Webster dictionary for the proper spelling of an abbreviation (see Rule 130). Capitalized abbreviations generally have no spaces or periods between letters (AIDS, ATM, IBM).  Lowercase abbreviations usually have no spaces with periods between letters (a.k.a., a.m., p.m.).  An abbreviation with an ampersand has no spaces (R&D).

Some Common Abbreviations:

| Abbrev. | Meaning |
| --- | --- |
| AD | Latin: *anno domini* from *anno domini nostri Jesu Christi* (in the year of our Lord). See below. |
| a.k.a. | also known as |
| a.m. | Latin: *ante meridiem* (before midday) |
| ASAP | as soon as possible |
| BC | before Christ |
| BCE | before the common era (see below) |
| CE | common era (see below) |
| CEO | chief executive officer |
| Co. | company |
| Corp. | corporation |
| d/b/a | doing business as |
| DOB | date of birth |
| e.g. | Latin: *exempli gratia* (for example). See below. |
| ETA | estimated time of arrival |
| etc. | Latin: *et cetera* (and so on). See Rule 193. |
| FY | fiscal year |
| i.e. | Latin: *id est* (that is). See below. |
| mph | miles per hour |
| OTC | over the counter |
| p.m. | Latin: *post meridiem* (after midday) |
| Q&A | question and answer |
| SSN | social security number |
| U.S. | United States (see below) |

Abbreviate *United States* as "U.S." (with periods), not "US" (without periods).

The abbreviations BCE and CE, instead of BC and AD, are widely used in academic fields, especially archeology, history, and theology. Most style guides do not use periods (BC and AD), but The *Associated Press Stylebook* and *The Gregg Reference Manual* use periods (B.C. and A.D.).

For *e.g.* (for example) and *i.e.* (that is), follow Rule 45 where a semicolon is generally used before the abbreviation and a comma after.

- The offer lacks a basic title; e.g., "Offer to Build a House."
- The offer lacks things; i.e., an itemized cost estimate, a schedule, and a contact number.

## Rule 193. Only Abbreviate These Words

Do <u>not</u> use any abbreviations unless spoken. The exceptions to this rule are the following:

| | |
|---|---|
| Before a name: | Dr., Mr., Mrs., Ms., or Mx. |
| After a name: | Jr., Sr., or Esq. |
| After a year: | BC, AD, BCE, or CE |
| After a time: | a.m. or p.m.  (Rule 172) |
| In a legal citation: | v.  (Rule 132) |
| In a numbered reference: | No. or Nos.  (Rule 183) |
| In an address: | street or state name with limited space or on envelope (Rule 177) |

Do <u>not</u> abbreviate *okay* as *OK* or *ok*.

Do <u>not</u> abbreviate *et cetera* as *etc*.

The best practice for the word *Saint* in a place name is <u>not</u> to abbreviate (use Saint Louis, not St. Louis).

Examples:

- Will Ms. Hailey Anderson, Esq., attend the company dinner with Mr. Thomas Smith Sr.?

- The email stated, "Dr. Cooper cannot attend the company dinner this Friday at 5:30 p.m. in Saint Helena, California."
  - Or: stated: "Dr. Cooper  (see Rule 75).

- For this study of volcanos by Dr. Stevenson, Eruption No. 56 is the 1980 eruption of Mount Saint Helens.

- Okay. What time did you leave?
  - Not:  OK or ok.
  - See Rule 4 for using a period after *okay* at the beginning of a sentence.

- The items in the moving van included beds, boxes, furniture, et cetera.
  - Not: etc.
  - See Rule 14 for using *et cetera* in a series of items.

See Rule 102 for creating certain verb forms (ID'd).

**Rule 194. Title or Professional Degree After a Person's Name**
Do <u>not</u> use periods in a title or professional degree after a person's name.

- Rebecca Farley, DDS, extracted the tooth.
- We spoke to Mr. Smith, PhD, for more information.
- Michelle Wu, PE, is an expert in suspension bridges.

Using periods in a title or professional degree after a person's name was traditional usage (M.D., D.D.S., Ph.D., and so on). It is still used in newspapers (*Associated Press Stylebook*).

**Rule 195. Plural of an Abbreviation**
Form the plural of a capitalized abbreviation by adding *s*. Form the plural of a lowercase abbreviation by adding an apostrophe and *s*.

- Pat sold three TVs today.
- How many IOUs before a person says enough?
- The software blocked 17 suspicious URLs.
- The email had eight cc's and two bcc's.

**Rule 196. Possessive of an Abbreviation**
Form the singular possessive of an abbreviation by adding an apostrophe and *s*. Form the plural possessive by adding *s* and an apostrophe.

- After the news, IBM's stock price jumped 4 percent.
- The PhDs' combined knowledge could not explain it.
- That is only Tim Lew, Esq.'s opinion.
  - Omit the comma after the possessive of a title or degree (see Rule 91, Rule 25, and Rule 34).

**Rule 197. Letter to Represent a Last Name**
When a letter is used to abbreviate someone's actual last name, use a period after it.

- What happened after Ms. S. sold the boat?
  - *Ms. S.* abbreviates an actual last name.
- You said you sold the boat to Mr. X, right?
  - *Mr. X* does not abbreviate an actual last name, so no period after the letter.